TRENDOLOGY

This page intentionally left blank

TRENDOLOGY

Building an Advantage through
Data-Driven Real-Time Marketing

CHRIS KERNS

TRENDOLOGY

Copyright © Spredfast, Inc., 2014.

Softcover reprint of the hardcover 1st edition 2014 978-1-137-47955-6

First published in 2014 by
PALGRAVE MACMILLAN®
in the United States—a division of St. Martin's Press LLC,
175 Fifth Avenue, New York, NY 10010.

Where this book is distributed in the UK, Europe and the rest of the world,
this is by Palgrave Macmillan, a division of Macmillan Publishers Limited,
registered in England, company number 785998, of Houndmills,
Basingstoke, Hampshire RG21 6XS.

Palgrave Macmillan is the global academic imprint of the above companies
and has companies and representatives throughout the world.

Palgrave® and Macmillan® are registered trademarks in the United States,
the United Kingdom, Europe and other countries.

ISBN 978-1-349-50243-1   ISBN 978-1-137-47956-3 (eBook)
DOI 10.1057/9781137479563

Library of Congress Cataloging-in-Publication Data

Kerns, Chris.
    Trendology : building an advantage through data-driven real-time
    marketing / Chris Kerns.
        pages cm

        1. Marketing. 2. Internet marketing. 3. Social media. I. Title.
HF5415.K457 2014
658.8—dc23   2014023874

A catalogue record of the book is available from the British Library.

Design by Newgen Knowledge Works (P) Ltd., Chennai, India.

First edition: November 2014

10 9 8 7 6 5 4 3 2 1

CONTENTS

This page intentionally left blank

FIGURES

FOREWORD

HERE'S A FUN WAY TO START A LIVELY debate next time you find yourself sharing beers with a bunch of marketers: Ask them what they think about real-time marketing.

At *Ad Age*, we've thought (and written) quite a lot over the past couple of years—879 things, according to Google. We've pleaded with marketers to resist the instinct to just say something, anything, about the news of the moment. We admonished after a few truly awful Royal Baby-related attempts that "real time marketing is no longer about getting credit for just showing up." We've reminded marketers that not every time is the right time for real-time marketing, criticizing content about the anniversary of 9/11 as "inane at best and insensitive at worst."

But we've also held up smart examples, such as Tide, which saved $4 million by eschewing a Super Bowl TV spot and instead capturing people's attention with a series of smart Vines during the 2014 game. We praised Under Armour's real-time response to the speed-skating uniform controversy during the last Winter Olympics. We chuckled at J.C. Penney's clever #TweetingWithMittens Super Bowl stunt, and we crowned the Tweet that really kicked off the real-time marketing discussion in earnest—Oreo's "You can still dunk in the dark" response to a blackout at the 2013 Super Bowl—as "arguably the best ad of the game."

As a journalist, I believe a healthy dose of skepticism is never a bad thing, and every marketing tactic should have to earn its seat at the table.

The good news is that someone has finally dissected the data to prove that real-time marketing, in general, does. Chris Kerns looked across 100 brands to answer the question "Does it work"? The data-driven approach is a welcome one in a world where way too many brands have adopted the practice because, well, everyone else is doing it.

But it's not enough to prove the strategy works; brands also have to execute it well. That involves taking the time to develop guardrails, a brand voice, and a process for reacting more quickly. It's about listening more than talking. It's about building into the organization an expectation of agility. And it's about adopting a goals-driven approach that uses data not only to prove its worth day in and day out but adjust and optimize the strategy, learning from every piece of communication.

There's still a lot we don't know about social media. But here's what we do know: today's consumers are increasingly having conversations across digital media. These conversations are with each other, but they're open to hearing from brands as well. Brands, however, must give people a reason to care about what they're saying and a reason to share it.

The best real-time marketing feels natural, like it's meant to be there. When done well it has huge rewards in terms of boosting followers and engagement. But it's not just about big events like the Super Bowl or Oscars night; it's also about capitalizing on the daily zeitgeist, the things that are unexpected or unplanned for.

In the end, real-time relevance is much bigger than simply what brands are saying on Twitter—it's a philosophy that should be considered throughout a brand's communication.

It's not easy to get right, but it is essential for a twenty-first-century brand.

ABBEY KLAASSEN
Associate Publisher, Editorial & Audience
Advertising Age

ACKNOWLEDGMENTS

A BIG THANKS TO ALL OF my friends and colleagues that helped with every step of this book. Especially Amber Quist, Samantha Subar, Jim Rudden, Rod Favaron, Kevin Dasch, Manish Mehta, William Griggs, Marissa Sternberg, Meghan Shannon, Courtney White, Ashley Menger, Gordy Quist, Erik Qualman, Sam Decker, Ellie Falcao, Dan Doman, Monica Cravotta, Chris Clements, Ami Plasse, Adrianne Gallman, Lindsay Braun, Ross Gebhart, Dustin Blanchard, Chad Costello, Rachel Jamail, Brittany Edwards, Kate Merritt, Courtney Doman, Sarah DeRocher Moore, Andrew Chen, and Patrick Barrett.

I'd like to thank the thought leaders from across the industry who took time out of their busy days to be interviewed for this book, including Rebecca Lieb, Jim Sterne, Barry Cunningham, Josh Martin, Rod Strother, Peter Stringer, Sloane Kelley, Manish Tripathi, Michael Tai, Shawndra Hill, and Jason Burby. I'd like to thank my editor at Palgrave Macmillan, Laurie Harting, for her great guidance and support.

I'd like to thank the creators of the following Python packages and open-source tools that I used in data gathering and analysis for their awesome work: Pandas, Matplotlib, Twython, Numpy, NLTK, Gephi, and iPython.

And most of all, thanks to my wonderful family—Susanne, Zoe, and Sam—for all of their support and for letting me take time out of our lives to write chapters and analyze data on nights and weekends. You are awesome and funny and amazing and perfect.

CHRIS KERNS
August 2014

This page intentionally left blank

AUTHOR'S NOTE

REAL-TIME MARKETING IS A TREND THAT continues to evolve. To learn more about the newest advances in RTM, offer your views, and discuss the concepts in this book please visit:

http://www.TrendologyBook.com

and

http://www.chris-kerns.com.

You can also chime in on Twitter using the hashtag #Trendology

This page intentionally left blank

Introduction

NO TIME LIKE
THE PRESENT

SOMEWHERE IN SANDY SPRINGS, GEORGIA, a carpenter is hard at work. That carpenter is crafting something that can only be described as unique—a display case that will soon sit in the lobby of Arby's global headquarters. It won't house a trophy or a football helmet. It won't display a collection of "Employee of the Month" plaques. No, it's going to hold something much, much different. It will hold, believe it or not, a hat. A funny-looking hat. A hat that has only been worn a handful of times. But it might be the only hat in history that caused hundreds of CMOs to say "Why aren't we doing that?"

How it ended up in the hands of Arby's is now the stuff of social media legend. Months before, Josh Martin was sitting at home with the television tuned in to the Grammys. He had his laptop open, as he usually did for big events, to keep an eye on mentions of his employer's brand and anything else interesting going on. Josh leads social media for Arby's and was used to working during big events. His team had been prepping for this for weeks—getting approvals for different approaches and strategizing social media tactics to use, based on events during the show. But even Josh couldn't predict what was about to happen, and that he was about to write a Tweet that would change his life.

All of a sudden, during the preshow red carpet, it was clear that something out of the ordinary was happening. Josh noticed a large number of mentions about Arby's and the Grammys in his data feed. Arby's wasn't a big sponsor or involved in the event, so what was the connection between the fast-food chain and a music awards show? What was going on?

As Josh dove into the data, he noticed that a number of people were mentioning the hat worn by pop star Pharrell, and how much it resembled the Arby's logo. Josh and his team had prepared for the Grammys in order to make their mark on social media—just as they'd prepped for every big event that year. They had spent weeks preparing content for the event, running through scenario planning, and building out good, polished assets that could correspond to hundreds of things that could happen at the Grammys. But Josh had a new idea. Within 60 seconds, he wrote Arby's latest Tweet, right there on his couch.

Josh decided to ask for his hat back.

Josh posted the Tweet (Figure 0.1) just as Pharrell walked on stage at the beginning of the show, and Twitter exploded. Followers retweeted and favorited the content in record numbers. Pharrell himself tweeted back ("Y'all tryna start a roast beef?"), and the trend continued gaining steam. Josh brought his team together and discussed a reply, but the team decided that Pharrell's response was so good that the team should just leave it at that. Other brands chimed in, crowning Arby's the "social winner"

 **Arby's** ✔
@Arbys

☼   +⚊ Follow

Hey @Pharrell, can we have our hat back? #GRAMMYs

↩ Reply   ↻ Retweet   ★ Favorite   ••• More

RETWEETS   FAVORITES
81,452   48,306

7:28 PM - 26 Jan 2014

of the Grammys even before the event was over. Arby's had their day in the sun, and as far as they knew, they'd leave mentions of the hat behind them and move on to the next big event.

That is, until a few weeks later, when Pharrell decided to put the hat up for auction on eBay.

When the Arby's team learned the hat was available, and that the money would be going to a charity that looked to end child hunger (a cause that closely aligned with Arby's own corporate giving strategy), they made a business decision to purchase the item and keep the conversation going. When Pharrell tweeted and thanked the anonymous buyer, Arby's revealed its identity, via Twitter, and received another 10,000 retweets and 7,500 favorites. And those Tweets just happened to come during one of the other largest events of the year, the Oscars.

So how is it that Arby's, after only a few Tweets, saw over 100,000 total shares and 70,000 total favorites of their social content? How did Arby's see more than a 800 percent increase in social mentions of their brand in one day? How did Arby's become America's media sweetheart—the new leader in leveraging the power of social media? And how did a funny-looking hat gain enough worldwide attention to earn its own custom-made trophy case?

Welcome to the world of real-time marketing.

THE CONVERSATION IS SHIFTING

It wasn't that long ago when the only people creating content on social networks were…people. The thought of a brand having a presence on a social channel seemed foreign to most. People aren't there to talk to brands, they said. It will kill the whole channel, turn it corporate. When brands move in, ads will follow, and the conversation will seem too out of place. It will ruin the experience, they said. It will never work.

Turns out "they" were wrong.

Companies began to experiment. They started learning what works and what doesn't, and along the way they have turned social media into something that actually makes sense for a brand's bottom line. While social was new and exciting for brands, it came with its own set of challenges. Social was a new skill to learn, one that required experience, tools, and process, but the new kid on the block had some potential. Social brought unique opportunities that other channels couldn't begin to compare with. Pioneering brands —companies like ESPN, Nike, and McDonalds—learned that social could be an effective way to increase reach, get the audience involved, and be more creative.

But wait a minute. We have to...talk to our audience? Consumers can just send us a message that the whole world can see? They can complain about product defects and tell customer service horror stories for all to see? And we, as a brand, have to figure out how to respond, like, within a few minutes? And without pissing off legal? And without promising something we can't do? Who on earth would sign up for that job? What have we gotten ourselves into?

Brands quickly figured out that social isn't the same, or as easy, for a brand as it is for an individual. As an individual, you know your voice. You know which jokes you should and shouldn't make (for the most part), and which topics you want to discuss in a public forum. For a brand, each one of those decisions could easily be a 15-person meeting versus a gut reaction. You want Marketing, Legal, Product, and PR all to weigh in, and to receive executive approval. You have a distributed team of ten social media marketers all trying to field the same question or post on the same topic. It's chaos. *CHAOS.*

But brands quickly learned that the elements of social that were so difficult and intimidating at first are now becoming a crucial piece of what makes social so powerful. Conversations with customers require a lot of upfront planning, social media tools, and infrastructure, but can be more persuasive than traditional advertising. Conversations on social channels can target specific demographic groups and allow the audience to share and engage with your brand and campaign. Social can give a brand humanity, relevance, personality, and the ability to react to real-time events in a relevant manner. That's why real-time marketing (RTM) is possible, and why so many brands are jumping on board.

Fast-forward to today, and brands are as much of a part of major social networks like Facebook, Twitter, and Instagram as the personal connections that originally sparked the growth of the networks. More importantly, the presence of brands has opened the door for paid social advertising, which has become a huge revenue stream for these now all too often public companies. Social networks build out advertising opportunities for companies to get in front of this engaged audience and bring in billions of dollars in ad revenue for their efforts. Today, social networks roll out innovation to ensure that brands feel welcome on their properties, hoping to attract larger and larger pieces of ad spend budget in future years. Brands have responded by not only increasing their ad budgets on social networks but by increasing their participation in everyday conversation as well. As brands have grown alongside the social networks, they've learned a thing or two about what works on these new channels.

Companies now understand that finding success in social requires playing by a new set of rules. They can't just repurpose assets used in outdoor advertising or on television—like messaging promoting a new summer sale or the video from a new beer commercial—and expect huge results from posting the exact same content on Instagram. In addition to bringing in different, and oftentimes, more valuable demographics, social media is also accompanied by a whole new set of expectations about the user experience. Companies have spent decades learning how to shout at their customers, how to build the best-performing one-way conversations that money can buy. But social has changed that. Now companies need to be reactive as well. Brands can talk directly to customers on social media, responding to their gripes and their love letters, even having fun with their customers. They talk about how their day was, ask what they had at Taco Bell for dinner, and say please and thank you. Brands are being humanized through social media because the social teams who are powering their brand voice have been given a longer leash. And as the sterile, traditional, old-school artificial walls fall down, customers respond and engage with companies more and more.

Smart companies are adapting to learn the strategies and tactics that work on these channels, and it's an ever-changing story with every new platform. Your audience on Twitter expects different messaging than it does on Facebook. Brands on Instagram and Snapchat need to understand the benefits and constraints of each channel and design content accordingly. And not only do the channels deserve different creative treatments but there is also one other big factor in play: timeliness.

CATCHING UP WITH REAL-TIME

Companies have traditionally been in control of their timing—when they want to put a message out into the market, how long that campaign will last, and when they expect to see a return for their efforts. But with more time and attention spent on social media, brands now have to adapt messages to fit the expectations for each social platform. The challenge with social is that it's based around conversations, trends, and things happening today. How, as a brand, can we predict the top five headlines that everyone will be talking about tomorrow? How do we get in on that conversation?

Brands need to alter their communication style to fit in with the mind-set of a social consumer. To do it right requires a balance of art and science. To do it wrong is pretty painful to watch.

Here's a completely made-up scenario, but one that happens every day:

Dave's Tweet: 12:35 p.m.

"Anybody in Austin for the ACL festival this weekend? Know where I can get good breakfast tacos? #hungry #tacoTuesday"

Rob's Tweet: 12:36 p.m.

"Can't wait to land in Austin and explore for ACL this weekend! #ATX"

Brand X's Tweet: 12:37 p.m.

"Good morning, everyone! What's your favorite flavor of Brand X's Chips? Tell us and RT! #ATX"

Susanne's Tweet: 12:38 p.m.

"Matt & Kim are playing #ACL this weekend, can't wait to see them on the main stage! #Austin"

Do you see what just happened? Everyone was talking about Austin City Limits, and then a brand jumps in with a crummy commercial.

Nobody's going to pay attention to that Tweet, and it doesn't mean that your customers don't love your brand or product. It's just the wrong time and place for the message. It simply doesn't fit in with the context of the conversation. The brand is talking about *their* agenda, while everyone else is on a *different subject altogether*. Brand X just became the guy at the party you regret starting a conversation with. He's going to come back from a quick trip to the bathroom to find only an empty keg and a random dude sleeping on the couch—everyone left without him, and, yes, he deserved it.

As brands become more conversational, they have to adapt their messaging and processes to match how conversations function. Conversations don't work well when you don't know what other people are talking about. Conversations are all about understanding what people are talking about *and then talking about the same thing*, using your opinion, voice, and experience. Sure, you have a message to get across. Sure, you have an agenda, but you need to blend that into the conversation. Because, as humans, that's what we expect, right?

To keep up with the social conversation, companies must understand what topics are being discussed, which ones are relevant for their brand to chime in on, and when the right time is to just sit back and be quiet. Makes sense – but easier said than done.

THE NEW TREND

Luckily, social media channels provide a vehicle for finding trends of conversation that are changing every minute, and are easily discoverable by both the audience and brands looking to have a say. Social teams have learned that when lots of people are talking about a topic, a brand can chime in to earn a seat at the table as long as they don't push it. And, yes, just like we saw above, your audience knows when you're pushing it.

Brands have learned that if they can build out a plan to create something poignant, clever, insightful, or funny to say about a topic, it can earn them a great response from the social audience. It's absolutely possible for brands to create social campaigns with a direct path to revenue, but most social efforts are a longer sell. A good social program can build the brand as an authentic voice and allow them to gain likes or followers so the brand can be heard more with future messaging and offers. It can allow the brand to come alive in ways that a billboard can't. It may not sell something to the consumer right at that moment, but neither does a television spot or a sponsorship, or even a good customer service experience. What it does is build the brand and increase the probability for sales in the future.

Real-time marketing is based on the idea that when the world's attention has shifted to a certain subject, it takes a lot of energy to try shifting it back to your agenda, your talking points, your story line. Why not use that energy to drift behind that topic of the day (or hour, or minute) and grab a piece of that attention for your brand?

HOW WE'LL LOOK AT RTM

As we'll explore in this book, real-time marketing has become an important step in the evolution of many brands' social media strategy. It's become expected that many brands will take advantage of current events and trends to attract attention for their products and services. And with the real-time environment that social media provides, brands now have a new challenge on their hands—campaigns and messaging that used to be planned over the course of a few months now need to be planned, executed, and analyzed within minutes to make their brand relevant and part of the moment.

Brands are catching on to the power of RTM during big events and the huge reach it can drive. Brands are looking to take advantage of the large audience and steal a bit of that attention for their own agenda. But as we'll discuss, brands can also use the same tactics to fill in the gaps between big tent-pole events and take advantage of RTM's benefits *every single day*. The structure and framework we'll build can be used not only for the Super Bowl every year but for micro-events like what's trending on Twitter this morning, or the latest headlines that only have a shelf life of two hours.

With every new marketing strategy comes a familiar group of voices: those who go all-in claiming it's the second coming of marketing (with no data to back it up their theories) and those who mock the process and diminish it as a flash in the pan (also, as it seems, without data behind their opinions). Well, I'd like to do my best to squash those claims with this book. Instead of storming in with an opinion and a big megaphone, we'll use data and analysis.

This book will examine real-time marketing with data as our guide, to set aside the hype and determine what really works. We'll walk through the process of how to create a team, how to identify trends using a data-driven approach, and how to learn from others who execute real-time marketing every day.

More specifically, we'll dive into the performance data for RTM and see if the numbers back up going to all this trouble in the first place. Does having a war room set up for the Golden Globes result in better social performance for a brand? Does creating a program for every-day RTM make sense? We'll look at the data from over 100 brands and media companies to find out.

BRINGING ORDER TO CHAOS

I can hear you already: all these success stories we hear about—the Arby's Tweet above being one of the biggest—was a blue moon. It was a once-in-a-lifetime event that can't be duplicated. Brands can't create these types of responses from a social media factory. How can we bring order to what could easily be a chaotic process of rapid, creative production?

Critics of RTM are quick to point out that each real-time event has brands that win and lose, and they believe that the wins are due to luck that is impossible to replicate. It's a ploy by agencies to staff a team on Super Bowl Sunday, or it's a lottery ticket to try and get a mention in the *New York Times* the next day as the "social winner" of the event. Well, fret not, my marketing friend, there is a method to the madness.

Setting up a goals-driven approach—and bringing data into the process before, during, and after each RTM execution—can help make sense of all this. Real-time marketing is no different than any other marketing strategy you use today, and you should be setting goals and measuring performance. You should be testing what works and doesn't work. And what better way to learn than with good data to back up your efforts? Let other people in the industry keep debating whether RTM is a fad or something that only social media managers find interesting. You'll have metrics to back up your decisions and know the impact of your RTM efforts before you go to bed that same night.

I've been using data and strategy to define digital measurement strategies for over a decade. I've worked with some of the world's largest companies to define their digital measurement strategies. I've spent the past few years mining social data for insights on posting patterns, text analytics, geolocation, content effectiveness, and social connection analysis. With a data-driven approach to real-time marketing, you're more equipped to define goals, identify moments to take advantage of, understand what your competition is up to, and know how to improve after each event. By the time you finish this book, I hope not only that I've convinced you that real-time marketing works in most cases but that you'll have a plan to use data to make the most of the opportunity in front of you.

What will we cover over the next few hundred pages? Here's a quick overview:

CHAPTER 1—RELEVANCE IS TRENDING UP

We'll begin with a definition of real-time marketing and a brief history of how it all got started. Next, we'll walk through the spectacular growth trend that RTM is experiencing and talk about why social media is a great platform for real-time, relevant content from brands. We'll also walk through some of the challenges of real-time, and introduce the concept of leveraging in-the-moment strategies to make an impact every day.

CHAPTER 2—UNDERSTANDING BRANDS ON TWITTER

Here we'll walk through what success looks like in social media, and start looking through our first set of data to understand a baseline for brand behavior on Twitter. We'll gather data from over 250,000 Tweets from over 100 brands to show patterns and different tactics used by companies to make the most of the social platform. Which brands are getting the best response from their audience? What are the patterns in language, timing, punctuation, media, and hashtags that work for brands? We'll learn all about these topics, and gather some best practices along the way.

CHAPTER 3—RTM PERFORMANCE FOR BIG, KNOWN EVENTS

Here's where the real fun begins. With a better understanding of how brands are using Twitter on a daily basis, we'll now dive into real-time marketing patterns and performance. How does RTM during big events perform versus normal, daily brand messaging? Does tent-pole RTM work for every brand, or are there patterns to success for specific verticals? What are the tactics we can learn from analyzing language, influence, and connections to maximize brand RTM effectiveness?

CHAPTER 4—RTM PERFORMANCE FOR UNKNOWN EVENTS AND DAILY TRENDS

We'll continue our research in understanding the performance of RTM by looking at smaller events throughout the year as well as everyday trends. When brands jump on an everyday conversation that is trending with their audience, how does the performance stack up? What should brands be preparing for, and which events make brands work harder than others? We'll find out.

CHAPTER 5—LAYING A DATA-DRIVEN FOUNDATION FOR REAL-TIME

Building out internal capabilities for real-time response isn't accomplished on accident—it takes an experienced team, executive alignment, and much, much more. We'll build the foundation for our Data-Driven RTM Process by laying the groundwork for success.

CHAPTER 6—AIMING FOR REAL-TIME SUCCESS

Crafting a strategy begins with establishing the right goals and measurement. In this chapter, we will outline the best practices for building a usable, repeatable RTM measurement strategy that will propel brands toward success and optimize their tactics with each campaign.

CHAPTER 7—THE DATA-DRIVEN RTM PROCESS

Now that we've learned what works, this chapter will detail a plan to create an RTM methodology that includes data baked into every step. What are the best practices for People, Process, Technology, and Analysis for RTM? How can data give brands a huge advantage in every stage (in planning, execution, and post-campaign analysis) of the process? The result will be the go-to guide for building a data-driven, insights-fueled process for RTM.

CHAPTER 8—THE FUTURE OF RTM

Real-time marketing is just getting started. I'll explore the possibilities and opportunities I see for RTM as social networks and technology continue to evolve. Looking at new, emerging platforms and trends that are taking place, I'll evaluate what works and where gaps still exist, and present data to show which emerging trends are experiencing the most success.

So let's dive in and have some fun. We'll hear opinions from top people in the industry, look at social data in new ways, and plan out a strategy that works for your team.

Let's get to work.

Chapter 1

RELEVANCE IS TRENDING UP

TODAY ALL MARKETERS ARE LIVING IN A real-time world, but few are actually taking advantage of it.

Information travels fast, but new information travels faster—the topic of the day, the talking points, the newest biggest thing. It seems that information overload increases as fast as the technology designed to carry it—every year, every month, every day. As the latest headlines come and go, the attention of your audience goes with them. Wait...there's a breaking news alert on CNN. Hold on, I just got a text. Did you see that Beyonce is trending this morning? I wonder why, let me check. Let me just log into Facebook to see if there's something new since I last checked two minutes ago. I just got a Snap—let me just, ok, sorry, what were you saying?

Marketing has always revolved around attention. Where eyeballs, time, and awareness have traveled, brands and their messages have quickly followed. A message without an audience is a message that isn't heard, and brands have made it their business to know where potential consumers are listening, and where those trends are shifting. In the 1920s as the US interstate highway system was built out, Americans started hitting the open road and spending more time than ever in their vehicles, searching for their next adventure. As brands realized that the attention of their audience was suddenly hitting the pavement, they came along for the ride, and suddenly billboards appeared to keep Burma-Shave and Wall Drug in front of potential consumers. In the 1930s as listeners tuned in to popular radio shows like *Little Orphan Annie*, Ovaltine was there with radio spots to capitalize on the ears and minds that were hanging on every story line in every house, every week. As attention turned to television, and decades later with the Internet, ads have followed suit. And now that people in the United States spend an average of *37 minutes a day* on social networks, advertisers are happy to jump on board with properties like Twitter and Facebook as well.

But marketers know that just getting in front of their audience isn't enough—they also need something to say that resonates with listeners. Advertisers need campaigns and messages that not only keep up with the times but also take advantage of relevant topics to grab attention. Seeing Psy (that's the Gangnam Style guy) in a Super Bowl ad a few years ago wasn't a mistake; rather, it was a marketer trying to capitalize on a current and widely recognized trend via brand association. Connecting to that existing reference has value for the brand, and marketers will pay handsomely for the rights to appear modern and pertinent. But trends do not last forever, and as fashion, music, and other pop culture staples shift, brands adjust their imagery and creative to stay relevant.

In the past, fads lasted for months and years, even if they shouldn't have—like Hypercolor shirts or Pauly Shore. Trends and topics would stay top of mind for long periods of time and provide a more predictable road map of topics for the company to leverage. But in the digital age, 24-hour news cycles and social media have generated a new culture of micro-trends—fads and topics with a shelf life that can sometimes be measured in minutes. These topics are top of mind for a very short period of time, but thanks to today's quick dissemination of information, they still attract big attention from a brand's audience. What brands are discovering is that this new micro-trend culture offers a new marketing opportunity for those who are willing to innovate.

While the life cycle of new trends continues to shorten, the pressure placed on brands continues to mount. To add to the stress, these trends bring new channels for brands and media companies that require a new set of skills and tactics. You can't plan an outdoor campaign around a micro-trend that lasts 24 hours, or at least you probably shouldn't. Social isn't a billboard. It's a conversation. It's a completely different species of media—with its own set of opportunities and challenges. Knowing how divided, or even fleeting, the attention of our audience is today, smart marketers have found a new technique to maintain relevance in the minds of current and potential customers. It's an attempt to travel alongside customers as they shift with trends, and stay relevant with the audience as they spot the next thing that will grab their attention. This practice is called real-time marketing.

REAL-TIME MARKETING IS THE PRACTICE OF CREATING CONTENT INSPIRED BY A CURRENT TOPIC, TREND OR EVENT

As the world jumps from one topic to another, many brands and media companies are working to keep themselves in the spotlight. The realities of RTM contain many new pitfalls for companies, and the road gets a little bumpy as real-time topics are often unpredictable and highly diverse. This means RTM brands must be nimble. It means RTM brands need to understand their brand promise, values, and voice inside and out. And it means that RTM brands have to be prepared to jump on new opportunities every day.

Why on earth would anyone want to sign up for this?

Why? Simply put—because brands are seeing value in the practice.

TRENDS DRIVE RELEVANCE

Real-time marketing capitalizes on a trending topic with a timely message that strikes while the iron is hot. The result of this is relevance, which is the key driver to RTM's success and adoption. Whenever a brand's message can adapt to the mind-set of the audience and also have something interesting to say, the message will be heard with increased clarity and volume. Regardless of the tactics brands use to achieve this end result, relevance is still the core concept driving success.

Figure 1.1   Denny's Tweet after the 2014 BCS Championship Game

RTM is designed to take advantage of the attention surrounding a trending topic and redirect a portion of that attention back to a brand. Much like a NASCAR driver drifts behind his competitor, brands can use RTM to gain speed without exerting as much effort (or budget) to get a consumer's attention. If done right, they can easily grab impressions and reach that would otherwise have to be bought. Companies can still convey their brand identity and voice to many, many more consumers for a low cost of entry, and even use tailored offers to see real revenue from RTM.

Imagine the following scenario:

1. You're watching the Super Bowl and your favorite football team intercepts a pass from the other team. Did you see that? Did that really just happen? Shouts of joy fly from your mouth. Your dog

runs out of the room, frightened. Suddenly, everything is awesome.

2. You must share this excitement with the rest of the world, especially your friends rooting for the other team. Sure they are your friends, but during this game and only during this game, they are terrible people.

3. You take out your phone and open the Twitter app.

4. You post "*OMG damn straight #goPackers #interception,*" hit the "Send Tweet" button, and take a victory sip of your favorite beverage. Victory, as it's been told, tastes sweet.

5. As your see your post go live in the Twitter feed, you notice a few other people talking about the same topic. You start to wonder what the Twitterverse is thinking about the play. You do a quick search for "interception," and at the top a Tweet pops up from your local pizza place. "What are they doing on here?" you wonder in your slightly buzzed head. Reminder: at this point, it's only been about 30 seconds since that last play.

6. TonysPizzaPlace tweets "*Nice pick! Packers fans, pick your favorite pizza now for only $10. bit.ly/tonyspizza #interception*"

7. That's kind of clever, you think, and you hit the RT button. Maybe you'll order pizza at halftime, and if you do, you know you'll get a deal from Tony's. Back to the game.

That is real-time marketing at work—capitalizing on an event where a brand knows there will be attention and conversation, and grabbing a slice for themselves. How much did it cost Tony's Pizza Place to send that Tweet? Pretty much nothing, other than having a social media person monitoring the game, and an offer/link ready to go. What's the upside? As I'll show you via some data analysis later in this book, it can be pretty big.

But the impact of the above scenario isn't just getting in front of more eyeballs. It's about being relevant in the moment. Not only does Tony's Pizza realize that people will be watching the big game, they realize that the micro-event, in this case the interception, is what everyone is talking about for the next two minutes. By connecting their message to that event with the "pick your favorite pizza" line, which plays off the "pick" slang for an interception, it integrates with something that is already top of mind for the audience. Suddenly, Tony's Pizza is relevant to the conversation at hand, and not trying to distract their audience away from what they were already doing. The above scenario wouldn't have clicked with the audience at the same level if Tony's Pizza had tweeted, "What's your favorite pasta?" during the game. It's not just about timing, but a combination of the timing and the message.

The value of RTM goes far beyond just pizza places and consumer-packaged goods brands—plenty of media companies are reaping the rewards of real-time as well. News organizations are responding to trending topics to make sure their programming is relevant and in line with their audience's attention. Television shows use real-time polling and commentary from the audience to capture the voice of everyone watching and assure the audience that they have a say in the conversation. By using these tactics, media companies are leveraging real-time to connect with their audiences in new and innovative ways.

We're now seeing an explosion of RTM, mostly because social media is such a great medium for real-time messaging to reach the masses. But real-time marketing didn't just appear out of the blue—it's been happening in one form or another for years. Brands have recognized the value, but only recently acquired the tools and connectivity to execute RTM effectively.

TRENDING: THEN AND NOW

This new movement of brands engaging with the audience via social media channels isn't the first time we've seen real-time marketing in action. Companies have always known that if you can get yourself in the mind-set of the consumer, good things will follow. One example of this is a well-known saying that has lasted for a generation.

For years, Disney has paid the Super Bowl MVP to endorse their theme parks directly after the win, while the confetti is still flying.

"You just won the Super Bowl! What are you going to do now?"

"I'm going to Disneyland!"

Over the years, the punch line to this annual campaign has become an iconic saying throughout America. But it's not just smart marketing—it's also a great example of RTM. The commercials would air the next day in the early years, but by the time the '90s came around, the commercials were turned around so fast that they were televised that same night. Disney made their brand relevant by association—packaging the Super Bowl celebration and their brand together and sending it out to an already captive audience. And by jumping on a topical event in a timely fashion and tying their brand to that winning experience, Disney became a pioneer in RTM.

ONLINE: A BETTER UNDERSTANDING OF WHAT'S TOP OF MIND

Forms of real-time marketing have been happening for years on more traditional Internet properties, like Google. Google's huge market for AdWords, which brought in over $30B in revenue for them in 2013, capitalizes on knowing that searches show intent, such as intent to purchase an item ("Converse shoes") or understand more about a topic ("Spinal Tap quotes"). Google uses this search intent to optimize the advertisements put in front of the user while they are top of mind. For example, if I performed the "Converse shoes" search above, Google would know that I have some level of interest in knowing more about shoes and even possibly buying shoes. Not only does Google know that, but it knows that I am particularly interested in the Converse brand. So Google not only serves up the best natural search listings (Converse.com, the Wikipedia page on Converse), it also displays paid search results for Zappos's or Converse's e-commerce site right at the top of the page. Because the search topic is top of mind for me, I'm much more likely to click on those ads to learn more about or buy the shoes right now versus look at a banner ad that doesn't resonate with what's on my mind right now (like a Hawaiian vacation). It's no surprise that returns for both Google and the brands buying these ads perform much better than more traditional, noncontextual advertising. It's an adaptive form of advertising that wraps itself around the user's current state of mind versus the other way around. It's the right message in the right place at the right time.

More recently, the retargeting craze has repeated Google's success on other channels. By performing a search on "glasses," I show my intent that I'm in the market to upgrade my frames or lenses. Advertisers understand this, and now have the ability to follow me across multiple sites, prompting me with banner ads showing products that I've recently searched for or viewed. Instead of getting a random ad for something that I'm not interested in, I get one redirecting me back to Warby Parker—reminding me about my past intent. Come check out these frames you just looked at. Bring your attention back where it was a few days, hours, minutes ago. Retargeting, like AdWords, results in better performance as compared to traditional advertising, all because of its real-time nature and an understanding of the value that attention can bring. It allows advertisers to understand your current mind-set, and advertise accordingly.

SOCIAL: THE REAL-TIME DESTINATION

So, yes, real-time marketing has seen success by innovative brands in the past few decades, but nothing like what we're seeing today. As it turns out, social media is what brands needed for real-time marketing to really take off, and it's no mistake that RTM efforts have exploded with the pervasive nature of social media in our modern lives. RTM gained huge momentum with our newest increase in real-time connections for a reason, but first let's recall a moment that helped start this growing phenomenon.

Let's jump in our social media time machine and send ourselves back to Super Bowl Sunday, 2013. Back then you had probably hadn't heard of real-time marketing, you had no idea the Pope was about to resign (or that he was even allowed to do that), and Edward Snowden still got along with the NSA just fine. It was a simpler time.

And, if you're working for a brand or agency social media team, you're actually at home enjoying the big game with friends and family. I call these "the good old days."

Suddenly, right after the game starts back up post-halftime, the lights go out in the Superdome. What on earth just happened? Is everyone seeing this? You check Twitter, and then one of the most famous (and most retweeted) Tweets of the year appears (Figure 1.2).

The next day, everyone's talking about the blackout, but more importantly, everyone's talking about Oreo and a few other brands (Audi, Duracell) that had social media teams at the ready to jump on the trend. They get featured in *Ad Age*. They end up winning trophies at fancy advertising banquets with open bars. Clients and bosses are very, very happy.

For real-time marketing, this was a game changer. But this was just a one-time thing. It couldn't be repeated. It didn't have any value. The year 2013 would be the year of real-time marketing, and then agencies and their respective budgets would move along like nothing happened. It didn't have any value, the pundits cried, so why would brands try to do it again?

Figure 1.2 The Oreo Tweet, from the 2013 Super Bowl, that opened eyes to the power of a good RTM program

So what happens when we fast-forward one year to the 2014 Super Bowl, and see what happened to this so-called social media "flash in the pan?" Well, if you worked on a social media team in the past few years, you'd probably know the answer to that already, and it involves working on Sundays.

MORE BRANDS FLOCKED TO REAL-TIME MARKETING

RTM adoption for brands listed in the Interbrand 100 grew year over year by more than 260 percent (Figure 1.4)—from eight brands in 2013 to twenty-nine brands in 2014.

Just to be clear, these aren't little mom-and-pop startups we're talking about here. The Interbrand Top 100 is a group of the top 100 most valuable brands in the world. In 2014, some of the real-time marketing newcomers were established corporations like Honda, Visa, Volkswagen, and Kia. These are big players with big budgets—brands that could easily afford a Super Bowl commercial. But many instead decided to invest in social, and specifically in real-time marketing.

When you step back, this shouldn't be all that surprising. Every article we read these days seems to be about a new social network, or an innovative agency building out sophisticated social media teams across

Charmin ✔
@Charmin   ⚙   +⚫ Follow

Is it too early to call this game a blowout?
#tweetfromtheseat

↰ Reply ⇄ Retweet ★ Favorite ••• More

RETWEETS   FAVORITES
44   36

6:38 PM - 2 Feb 2014

Figure 1.3   Charmin's social media team tweeting during the 2014 Super Bowl

	Super Bowl 2013	Super Bowl 2014	
Social Media Activity	37	41	+11%
Real-Time Marketing	8	29	+263%

Figure 1.4 Super Bowl RTM growth far outweighed overall Super Bowl social media activity growth by brands from 2013 to 2014

the globe. With more brands on social media, and more social channels to work with, the growth of RTM can probably just be explained by social media's overall growth from 2013 to 2014. But as you can see in Figure 1.4, there's no comparison.

Looking at the Interbrand 100 and their Super Bowl social activity from 2013 to 2014, there was indeed growth in brands posting during the show itself. In 2013, 37 percent of the Interbrand Top 100 posted some form of social media during the Super Bowl across Twitter, Facebook, or Instagram. In 2014, that number grew to 41 percent. So social media grew a bit, but nothing close to RTM's year-over-year growth. Or said another way—social media activity by top brands during the 2014 Super Bowl grew by 11 percent. RTM grew by more than 260 percent.

One notable brand that decided to bow out of the RTM spotlight during the 2014 Super Bowl was last year's shining star. Just before the game kicked off, Oreo tweeted, "Hey guys…enjoy the game tonight. We're going dark. #OreoOut." Rebecca Lieb, an analyst for the Altimeter Group covering digital advertising and media, thinks it was the best way for Oreo to handle the expectations facing them. "It was very interesting to see the brand that has become the poster child for RTM politely bow out of the Super Bowl, which I thought was a very good strategy on Oreo's behalf," Lieb said. "But it was also important to them to make a statement and not be entirely missing from the scenario and I think their approach was a very elegant one."[1]

If 2013 was the year RTM showed up, 2014 was the year it became legit. Real-time marketing, it seems, is making its way into boardrooms and budgets across the globe. Lieb sees global technology clients that are changing the way they manage their channels based on RTM. "I know one major technology brand that has just created different Facebook pages for different regions in the world. One of the reasons they elected to do this is real-time marketing. They know they will get more resonance from a real-time topic and they want to roll that out by geography to capture that momentum and velocity. Real-time is now being cited by marketers as a fundamental reason for segmenting."[2]

Last year, Lieb says, brands were more interested in pouring their budgets and attention into social listening, a technology to monitor levels of brand conversation on social networks. This year it has shifted into what she calls "scenario planning," which emphasizes preparing for rapid response to multiple possible outcomes, both positive and negative. "Brands have always needed disaster scenarios and planning, but I'm now seeing all marketing strategy and content strategy begin to ladder up to RTM, and have RTM baked into what large enterprise organizations are planning for. I am seeing more and more brands trying to build RTM into their social marketing and content marketing practices, strategy, and organizational structure."[3]

WHY SO SOCIAL? THE ADVANTAGES OF SOCIAL + RTM

So real-time marketing has been around awhile, but in the past few years it has really started gaining momentum with big brands and media companies. Why has RTM flourished on social media? What makes social the new go-to vehicle for engaging audiences in real-time?

The reasons are built into the very fabric of social platforms. Social media is fundamentally different from all previous marketing channels. While social channels don't necessarily fit with traditional advertising models, they have many dimensions that allow marketers to do things they've never done before. From its form factor to its measurability to the medium itself, social might seem like the perfect marriage for RTM. How so? Let us count the ways.

IT'S SHORT FORM

To grab attention during a live event, you're going to need to be quick and to the point. Writing a four-paragraph essay on why Daft Punk should have won that Grammy isn't going to cut it. People have a show to get back to. Not only does the audience not have time for long-form takes on real-time events, your team doesn't have time to create that much content and still keep up with the ever-changing conversation at hand. The short form of Twitter and Facebook works perfectly in this environment. And with embedded photos and videos, brands have lots of different ways they can engage with their audience. But remember—social shouldn't be a novel. Be quick, be engaging, be gone.

IT'S RELATIVELY CHEAP

Say what you will about agency costs and staffing an experienced social team—when you compare the cost of sending out a few Tweets to a Super Bowl ad, you're not even in the same ballpark. In fact, the low barrier to entry of social makes me wonder why every brand isn't doing some form of RTM today. The low cost of engaging in the moment on social media makes the strategy accessible for not only established brands but also for emerging brands and smaller mom-and-pop shops (like Tony's Pizza Place from our earlier example).

THE SECOND SCREEN IS EXPLODING

Social media usage in conjunction with major events is trending up every year. If customers are already on Twitter talking about the Oscars, it makes sense to go meet them there. Combine that insight with the second screen demographic, a predominantly younger audience that advertisers fight to get in front of, and you've got a very attractive opportunity for marketers. If you bring your brand and message to the location where the audience already lives, it will take less energy than sending them to your owned properties.

IT'S MEASURABLE

Impressions, engagement, clicks, shares. You know how well your social efforts are performing, and you get that information instantly. You don't have to wait for ratings to come out the next morning, or three months for the next quarterly focus group. Not only are the interactions real-time, but the analytics are real-time as well. Try doing that with a billboard, old marketing guy who's still selling billboards.

IT'S VERSATILE

Social is a platform that allows for many types of interactions—from posting of original messages to one-on-one conversations, including media such as images and short-form video, and including links to other content. Social can not only provide a rich canvas for your creative team but also offers unique tactics that can be used to grab a consumer's attention. As RTM has evolved over the past few years, we've seen a few interesting patterns emerge. Not only are brands trying to get the attention of consumers by talking about the micro-events during a large event, they are also reaching out to other brands through RTM efforts to create new story lines within events.

Brand-to-Consumer RTM

Posting content to followers around a trending topic. The purpose is similar to normal social posts, but differs with it's topical nature.

Brand-to-Brand RTM

Reaching out to other brands during a large event, typically brands that are also doing RTM for a tent pole event, with good-hearted content.

Figure 1.5 The differences between Brand-to-Consumer and Brand-to-Brand RTM

I know I probably lost you right there, so I'll try to break this down with a bit more clarity. RTM has branched out into two forms: *brand-to-consumer* and *brand-to-brand*. We can define these as the following:

Brand-to-consumer RTM is what you might expect from a brand, with messages that are meant to resonate with the entire audience. Did something big just happen in an awards show? A brand can chime in on this trend and give their congratulations, express disappointment, or make fun of the acceptance speech. Is #USA trending today on Twitter? Brands can chime in to show their patriotism and stay on topic with a large audience.

Brand-to-brand RTM is a new form of communication that tends to happen mostly, but not exclusively, during big events. This is when brands decide to call each other out on a social network, and it can take many different forms. It can include one brand congratulating another on a funny or effective RTM piece of content during an event. It can be a brand surprising another with a message, hoping the other brand joins in and that both brands can benefit from the increased exposure. It becomes part of a larger sideshow: when Tide makes fun of JC Penney, it makes followers interested to see what might come next.

Brands that use brand-to-brand RTM are typically also doing brand-to-consumer RTM at the same time. I haven't seen any brands try for a strictly brand-to-brand RTM strategy, which could prove to be kind of awkward if the other brands aren't responding. Ultimately, the goal of brand-to-brand communication is still about engaging consumers, but also getting them involved in the "back room" conversations between brands.

We'll dive into the performance of brand-to-brand RTM conversations, and whether the tactic has worked effectively to increase engagement—but for now, just know that it's a thing.

REAL-TIME MARKETING, REAL-TIME CHALLENGES

Now, there are some that claim real-time marketing is a magic bullet. Just jump on a few trends and your social media performance will take off. There's no other work to get done, and by the way you can manage the entire process from your pool. Sorry, Spicoli, it's not quite that easy.

I need to break the bad news and tell you that while RTM is a huge opportunity, there are still plenty of land mines you need to navigate. Many of the same attributes that make social a great place for RTM can also make it a challenging strategy to undertake. I've seen many brands attempt to jump into the game and fail miserably, and it's ugly when it happens. I'm not just talking about posts that I don't find personally engaging or amusing—I'm talking about posts that do a downright pitiful job at engaging their audience.

Fear not, RTM newcomers. I have categorized these misses for your knowledge and protection so you can steer clear of these social blunders. Here are a few missteps.

ACCEPTING THE NARRATIVE VERSUS SETTING THE NARRATIVE

In traditional advertising, you're creating a story about your brand and bringing your value proposition into that story. A brand defines a story to tell based on which aspects of the brand (quality, value, prestige, etc.) they want to drive home with consumers. When brands tell stories in advertising, they have control over where the story gets told, and which topics they believe will resonate with the audience.

With RTM, the story has already been set. People are talking about a certain topic that is top of mind, and it's the brand's responsibility to wrap their message around the existing context. If the brand wants to participate in the conversation, they'll need to create a memorable take on that current event and not just try to start a separate dialogue. Brands can control their own handling of the topic and craft a funny, insightful, or supportive message depending on the circumstance, but they need to stay within the brand voice and on topic. In some respects, this is an easier job for the social media team, and in other ways it presents its own unique set of challenges.

THE CLOCK IS TICKING

If you're looking to gain the benefits of jumping on trends, you'll need a team that has the ability to focus on the "real-time" aspect of RTM. Do you have something clever to say about Matthew McConaughey's acceptance speech at the Oscars? You'd better do it within a few minutes, or everyone will have moved on. You'll need a team ready to create, post, and analyze your efforts in real-time. Luckily, it's a pretty easy problem to solve with the right technology, processes, data, and structure.

BE PREPARED

So you think you're ready to get in there and play with the established RTM brands? Then you'd better leave your premade creative at home. You're not going to win any RTM battles sitting in the sandbox with off-the-shelf copy and creative. People can tell when you're faking it.

While you'll need flexibility and creativity to build content as new trends pop up, that doesn't mean you don't need to prepare. As a brand, you need to be ready when gearing up for real-time marketing. While some of the best RTM posts seem like they were created on the fly, there's actually a good amount of planning and preparation going on behind the scenes to take full advantage of each micro-event. Remember that old saying your Mom used to drill into your head: "Luck is what happens when preparation meets opportunity"? Turns out Mom was right.

IDENTIFYING THE RIGHT TRENDS

According to a 2014 CMO Club / Mass Relevance study, 95 percent of chief marketing officers say that finding new, timely, and engaging content is one of their biggest hurdles. Brands engaging in RTM can cast a wider net for finding topics and content to associate with their brands, but with an understanding that there is risk surrounding certain subjects. Today I'm seeing people talking about Justin Bieber on social networks. Should we chime in? Is that a subject we want to associate with our brand? Do we have something relevant to say? Finding the balance, and having a good set of guardrails established for your team regarding when to engage and when to stay away, is essential to a successful RTM program.

FINDING THE RIGHT CHANNEL

Another way to misfire on real-time marketing is posting to the wrong social network, or the social equivalent of bringing a knife to a gunfight. Marketers need to understand that all social channels are not created equal when it comes to the real-time environment. Hardly anyone is going to be watching your brand page on Pinterest during the Super Bowl, hoping you pin a new recipe. Pinterest does a lot of great things, but real-time isn't their killer feature. Make sure the social network you choose is right for the impact you're looking to see, and fits with the audience you're looking to target. And don't be afraid to experiment with some of the new emerging channels that are popping up every day. Audi did a great job using both Twitter and Snapchat during the 2014 Super Bowl, and got a good amount of attention for their efforts.

RTM OVERLOAD

I know, I know. When a big event comes up, you've been planning this day for a long time. You've got everyone working on a Sunday, the creative juices are flowing, and there is an endless supply of hilarious, clever banter ready to unleash on every social network under the sun. But you may want to pump the brakes a bit. Don't make the mistake of posting every other minute—remember, people who follow you may have every piece of content appear in their feed, and you don't want to assault them with an attack of death-by-social. Use restraint. Sometimes, less is more.

The challenges facing brands and media companies that are hoping to utilize real-time conversations are very real, but not insurmountable. Every strategy has its associated risks, and identifying them and building a risk management plan is the job of every manager out there. We've seen examples of brands that overcome these obstacles daily by building out strong teams with detailed planning. Instead of just shooting from the hip, these brands can balance risk and reward to gauge control of their outcome.

THE PEACOCK AND THE WOODPECKER

To get to know the ins and outs of real-time marketing, you can define and slice its use cases in many different ways. But the last thing I want to do is confuse you out of the gate, so let's talk about something simpler first. Let's talk about some of our friends from the animal kingdom, with a concept known as *the peacock and the woodpecker.*

The peacock is a bit of a show-off. The peacock is all about flash. The peacock picks a few select times to shine and goes big—spreading his huge feathers and showing off his wild colors for a flash, and then retreats until the next big event. And yes, the peacock gets noticed during his big reveal, but when those feathers go down, he kind of disappears until the next big thing.

Now, think about the woodpecker. The woodpecker doesn't have big, colorful feathers to work with. The woodpecker is small and out of sight and pretty unnoticeable except for one fact—the woodpecker is working every day. Tap tap tap. He's always out there, making some kind of progress, working toward a goal. Tap tap tap. He's not making a big deal out of what he's doing. He's just constantly tap tap tapping away, every day.

To make the most of your marketing efforts, you'll hopefully have a few peacock moments—big flashes of exposure and reach to make a big impact on your audience. But peacock moments are temporary and hard to achieve on a consistent basis. As a brand, you not only need large events to make your presence felt, you also need a constant rhythm of taps going on between big moments as well. You need to be a woodpecker (when you're not being a peacock) to keep yourself, and your message, top of mind.

What this means for real-time marketing is that you'll have your huge events—worldwide happenings like presidential elections, award nights—where you might look to make a big splash using real-time tactics. But there are not that many of those events per year, and RTM can continue to add value throughout the year, just like our good friend the woodpecker.

When we look at real-time marketing content over the years, it can be broken down into two main types of creative that stem from very different places. We'll call these known and unknown.

RTM for Known Topics

Known RTM content is meant to be posted in real-time as a large event is taking place, but it can be planned ahead of time due to the predictability around certain parts of the event. Brands know that the Super Bowl will have an opening kickoff, so when that happens, premade creative can be posted at the time of the micro-event.

RTM for Unknown Topics

Unknown RTM content can't be predicted, and therefore must be created in a reactive manner after a topic has become a trend. The blackout during the 2013 Super Bowl resulted in brands' creating content that they couldn't have predicted before the event. Creative teams quickly brainstormed, built, and posted in-the-moment social content.

If we combine both of these concepts—different types of events and known/unknown content, we get a model like we see in Figure 1.6.

The combination of topic predictability and event type give us a matrix with four quadrants. Let's walk through each.

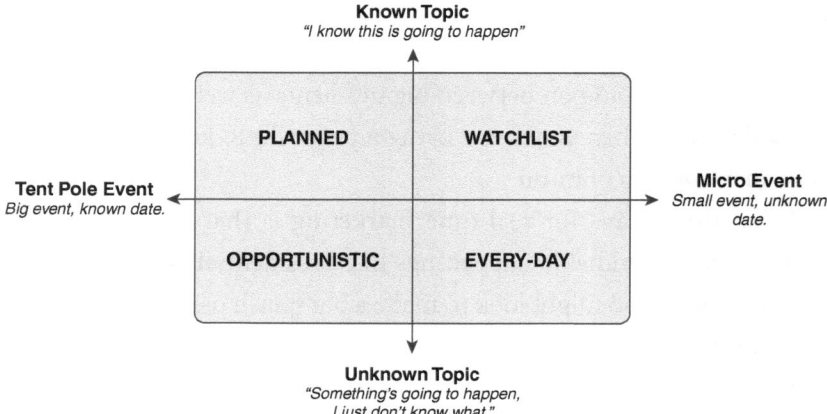

Figure 1.6   The Real-Time Marketing Matrix

Planned RTM

The Planned RTM quadrant represents a combination of known topics and a known event. Many facts about the Oscars are known weeks or months in advance—the date, the host, the nominees, the location, the start time, and so forth. Brands can plan content around these topics, knowing that they can build something predictable but timely well in advance of the show, like a Tweet proclaiming, "Here we go, the #Oscars just started!" just as the award show begins.

Watchlist RTM

The top right quadrant is where known topics meet everyday life. I refer to this as "The Bieber Quadrant," where we know that certain events will happen around a known topic, like a celebrity or political figure who is known to a large proportion of your audience, but we just don't know all the details around the topic, including what it is (which celebrities will get in trouble this week?) or when it will happen.

Opportunistic RTM

The bottom left quadrant includes micro-trends that pop up within larger events or, said a different way, the stories and topics that people are talking about as they are all discussing the same tent-pole event. The Super Bowl blackout of 2013 belongs in the Opportunistic RTM quadrant—it revolved around a foreseeable event (the Super Bowl) with lots of attention, but a topic (the blackout) that no one could have seen coming.

Every Day RTM

The bottom right quadrant is the Wild West of real-time marketing—trends that occur that no one could have predicted. This includes Twitter Trending Topics that appear out of the blue, and everything else that surprises us each and every day. The high-speed ebb and flow of micro-trends in this quadrant leaves many marketers scratching their heads on how to identify, quickly triage, and act on breaking stories.

TAKING A DATA-DRIVEN APPROACH

There are lots of opinions about real-time marketing—about whether it's worth a team's time to engage in the practice, and whether the practice is a trend that's here to stay. Media pundits and industry influencers have all chimed in, claiming to know whether RTM will succeed or fail. But for the most part, their opinions are biased, knee-jerk reactions, or at best a collection of anecdotal examples of a brand benefiting (or not) from their real-time efforts.

This is nothing new. As Michael Lewis detailed in the excellent *Moneyball*, the Oakland A's brought the practice of deep statistical analysis (also known as sabermatrics) to baseball, and were the first team to break the cycle of relying on gut instinct and outdated measurements to value available players. Other industries, including political analysts, venture capital firms, digital media companies, and even government agencies have all started taking data-driven approaches to understand more about every aspect of their business. They aren't doing this just because it's fashionable, or because they had a few extra data scientists sitting around; rather, they're doing it to gain an edge. Data can uncover hidden gems and unknown tactics that give companies an advantage. Data can help companies disrupt.

But to date, I haven't seen a data-driven analysis of RTM performance. Let's fix that.

HEY, MARKETER: YOU SHOULD LEARN HOW TO CODE

You should learn how to code. Yes, you. Now, don't throw the book (especially if you bought the e-book) across the room and grumble about having an MBA and that coding isn't your job. I have an MBA, too. And I'll write the code for you this time. *This time*. But next time, you should do it yourself.

I know what you're saying: "I don't have a computer science degree, dude, and I've seen the engineers that work here. I work on Madison Avenue, so I'm not going to start wearing sandals and t-shirts to work. Coders can stick to the coding. I'll stick to PowerPoint."

All good points. But I'm not saying you need to code for a living. You just need to know a little bit. Why? Because if you know how to write code, especially if you're a marketer, all of a sudden you have a *superpower*.

That's right, I said superpower. I've been working in analytics for a long time, and the off-the-shelf tools that are out there are getting better and better each year. They are great at answering the first question you have, and maybe the second question. But when you get deeper than that, the usefulness of the tools fall apart. They won't tell you what you want to know, and if you don't know how to work outside those tools, then you're stuck.

But if you're truly curious about your data, or if you want to combine multiple data sources to get a new view, your fancy tools will probably be of little to no help. And if you're like most people, when the tool can't give you the answer, you give up and just move on to one of the other 1,000 things on your plate. Or you send the request over to your Business Intelligence group, and maybe they'll get back to you in a few weeks. Or maybe they won't get back at all, because they already have too much work to do. And voilà, you just missed out on an opportunity.

Rewind a bit, and if you know the basics of coding, just a little bit of coding, you can answer those questions yourself, quickly, by building something to answer the question. And you don't need to start from scratch or have a PhD from Stanford to do it. These days, coding is different. Coding, dare I say, is much, much easier.

When I was a kid, I loved LEGOs. My brother and I would dump out giant boxes of blocks every day and build whatever we wanted, anything our little brains could conjure up. LEGOs were much more basic back then. There were few if any specialized pieces that already look like a boat or spaceship, but we could build off prebuilt elements (solid blocks for walls, seethrough blocks for windshields or windows, flat green pieces for grass, etc.) and make whatever we wanted—anything in the world.

Programming today is less about building things from a blank page, and more like putting LEGOs together. The language I code in, Python, is absolutely free, easy to learn, and has tons of free resources out there to help you. Thousands of people have gone through the process of learning Python from scratch, and many of them have written blogs about the easiest way for you to get from knowing nothing to getting things working. They've written how-to articles for every scenario you can think of.

Not only that, but more importantly there are thousands of prebuilt packages out there, built by the Python community, that you can download for free and use within seconds. Want to grab data from Twitter? There are lots of packages to do that. Do you want to build a web scraper to get information, programmatically, off of different sites from across the globe? There are many great ones already built, completely free, and completely documented. Want good frameworks for statistical analysis, graphing, social network analysis, text analysis, and pretty much anything else you can think of? You guessed it—they're all available, completely free, completely awesome, and could all be installed on your laptop five minutes from now.

And if you're a marketer, you have even more reason to learn. You can be the person who gets more out of your marketing data than anyone else on the team. The person who finally got a view of Salesforce data merged with Google Analytics data without having to pay out $100k to a vendor to do it for you. The person who analyzed sales leads and found out, via data, where to double down on ad spend. The person who isn't a programmer as their primary function, but uses their skill 5 percent of the time to get 10x the value out of marketing data. Not bad for someone that just learned how to code on the weekend.

Every piece of data analysis in this book was done with open-source (read: free) tools and public data. That means that *you* could have written this book.

So take it from me—do yourself a favor and learn a new superpower. Learn Python—and go play with LEGOs again. When you can play with your data via code, you'll start seeing it differently. You'll get to know your company better. You'll get to know your business better, and you'll be better at your job. You'll discover things that no one else knows. I guarantee it. Go make yourself a more valuable marketer—go learn how to code.

Data can change thinking that has existed for decades, and it can challenge theories that have relied on gut instinct. Data is not a replacement for creativity, but it's a catalyst to understand performance and give creative teams all the information they need to build the best plan to meet their goals. Data helps us set goals and track to those goals. And data helps us convince others—using more than just anecdotal examples—that our efforts are having a true impact and deserve resources and budget to support them.

WHERE DO I START?

Real-time marketing is taking off, but if you're new to the practice, where do you begin? Don't worry. That's why I wrote this book. When a new marketing trend emerges, brands all too often experiment by dipping their toes in the water without a plan in place. Brands and agencies do this without—and tears are welling up in my eyes as I type this—a data-driven approach for success. Well that's crazy talk, and I'm here to help.

Don't worry—I know that data analysis can be complicated and confusing. Setting goals and key performance indicators can be intimidating. Talking about the details of Python code and database structure and analysis isn't what you're here for, and, don't worry, it's not what I'll be diving into. But to figure out what's working, what's not working, and to make your brand a smarter social entity, we need to bring data into our daily lives. Data can help power your marketing efforts, and I promise I'll try to approach it in a user-friendly manner.

There are ways to manage the risk and take advantage of the opportunity surrounding RTM by using data. Data isn't going to write the perfect copy or photoshop Joe Flacco's head onto your brand mascot. Data won't guarantee your success with creating relevant content for your audience, but it will greatly increase your odds.

A data-driven approach to real-time marketing can help you to understand whether you succeeded or failed. A data-driven approach can help you understand what the competition does well (and does poorly, which is a lot more fun). Data can help you understand the right time to post, the right trend to jump on, and when the numbers tell your brand to *keep quiet*.

The key to RTM is to have it seem spontaneous, but actually be well orchestrated behind the scenes for optimal customer engagement, risk management, and brand positioning. Metrics can help with all of the above, and help you sleep a lot better not only the night of the big event, but the night before, too. And most importantly, it can help make every day a big event on social channels for your brand.

So what are we waiting for? Let's do this.

Chapter 2

UNDERSTANDING BRANDS ON TWITTER

IN THEIR INFANCY, SOCIAL NETWORKS WERE built around the value that exists in person-to-person communication. Depending on the channel, you saw content from friends, industry influencers, and celebrities that you chose to listen to and wanted to engage with. Social channels offered the opportunity to build new networks, stay informed, and discover new content like nothing before. Social networks changed the way you spoke to your friends and colleagues, and created an entirely new set of social rules for each new medium. The expectations for how your network was supposed to use Instagram were different from Pinterest and different from SnapChat. Users figured out the norms on each channel and expected others to do the same. People became acutely aware of what worked best, and learned the hard way (via unfriending and unfollowing) when they were stepping over the line.

Soon after, brands went through the same learning process as those first users, but now did so through the unique lens of a corporation. Companies found themselves in the same shoes as individual users once did—learning the expectations for each social channel and what was in and out of bounds. Could a brand talk about a subject that wasn't directly related to a product they sold? Was it ok for a brand to follow another brand? Was it ok for a brand to send Twitter followers 20 posts a day with the same offer (probably not)? In the beginning, no one was there with the answers, and innovative brands with a thick skin and an appetite for experimentation learned by doing.

Brands not only had to find the right patterns of when to post and how often to reach out to customers but also which messages, media, and timing worked best for what they were trying to achieve. Companies figured out their brand voice and tone—the right way to talk to an irate customer on Facebook, and what type of content should be retweeted. Brands built their social strategies piece by piece, and not all ended up looking the same.

In today's social world, social media teams create daily posts with brand messaging, campaign support, social-only offers, and other content using strategies that have been tested and refined over the years. It's rare that you visit your news feed or open your social app and not see some sort of brand messaging, whether it's organic brand content that you've opted to listen to or paid, promotional brand activity.

Brands have learned that social's ability to be real-time has both benefits and drawbacks. It's not uncommon these days to see someone on Twitter complaining to an airline about missing a flight—and then tweeting again just ten minutes later with even more anger due to a lack of response from the company. Expectations for real-time communication from brands and media companies are at an all-time high.

Some brands just want to have a conversation with you—to remind you on a daily basis that they are, or would like to be, part of your life (and, of course, top of mind for your next purchase.) Some brands, like Amazon, take the offer-only approach. The Amazon Twitter account Tweets out links to special offers on the site every day to over a million followers. Other brands, like Discovery Networks, send out interesting facts to curious social listeners. And DiGiorno's Twitter account really, really likes to talk smack. To each his own.

But even with all the diverse strategies, brand voices, and social tactics, patterns still emerge with how brands use social media. And if we use data in a smart way, we can find those patterns and learn from the best.

YO, THIS GAME IS LIKE A DIGIORNO PIZZA BECAUSE IT WAS DONE AFTER TWENTY MINUTES #SuperBowl #SuperSmack #DiGiorNOYOUDIDNT

Figure 2.1 DiGiorno's social media team, tweeting during the 2014 Super Bowl

BRANDS ON TWITTER—THE DATA

Let's stop talking anecdotes and start looking at some data. My end goal here is to see how real-time marketing stacks up against other social strategies that brands and media companies use every day.

But before we dive into an analysis of how brands are using RTM, let's first look at how they're using Twitter. Do brands just retweet other brands all day long, or are they actually creating their own content? What tactics do brands use that get them the best results? We'll aim to establish a baseline of performance that we can measure against different types of real-time marketing, and hopefully we'll learn something on the way.

For this baseline, we'll be looking at Twitter data, and looking for insights in the following areas:

- **Content types**: what is the typical makeup of brand Twitter content (original content, retweets and replies)?
- **Engagement**: which brands see the greatest engagement from their audience and why?
- **Time of Day**: what times during the day do brands usually Tweet? Does the time of day have any impact on Tweet performance?

- **Hashtags**: how do brands use hashtags, and what can we learn from this practice?
- **Text Analysis**: what language and punctuation do the top performing Tweets include?

Luckily, the Twitter public Application Programming Interface (API) is here to help. An API, said in civilian-friendly terms, is a way to get data out of a social network using a few lines of code versus having to look at every Tweet and write down numbers. The latter option sucks, trust me. You'd much rather be using APIs to get back structured, formatted data that makes it easier to slice, dice, and ultimately answer the questions you have.

In most books, this is the point where the author would start explaining how to access the Twitter API using a specific Python package, making sure to use your consumer key and access token, and how to parse through the JSON response. Don't worry—we're not going to do that here. I'll write the code and grab the data, and we'll walk through the findings from a few different angles. It will all be as user-friendly and child-safe as possible. Did we just become best friends? Yep.

THE COMPANIES

So what's the best way to look at brands and media companies using Twitter today? We could look at a random sample of companies that happen to be top of mind this week, but that's not a very thoughtful or insightful way to approach the exercise. What we should be interested in is how some of the biggest, most innovative brands in the world are working with social media today.

To accomplish this, I started with the Interbrand 100 list from 2013.[1] This is a list of the most valuable brands in the world, brands that truly get marketing and how to build a brand that creates real, measurable value. The Interbrand 100 includes companies like Google, Coca-Cola, IBM, Microsoft, and GE. These aren't small little upstarts—these are giant companies that know how to make money by building a strong, reliable, innovative brand in the marketplace. Not only are they well-known brands, they are also social brands—98 of them are active on Twitter, making this list the perfect starting point for our study.

In addition to the Interbrand 100, I wanted to include enough data in our analysis to make sure we had a solid sample of real-time marketing content. I chose eight brands that have engaged in a good amount of real-time marketing during large events (like the Oscars, the Super Bowl, etc.) over the past few years to add to our study. Those brands are:

- **Arby's**—loves Pharrell's hat
- **Charmin**—seems to have a social team at the ready for every big event
- **Denny's**—never afraid to try new things with social
- **DiGiorno Pizza**—one of my favorite brands that was tweeting during the 2014 Super Bowl
- **Gain**—experimenting with RTM effectiveness in the consumer packaged goods (CPG) vertical
- **JCPenney**—made waves with their 2014 Super Bowl "Tweeting with Mittens" micro campaign
- **Oreo**—this one should be obvious by now
- **Tide**—great social team doing a lot of RTM in 2014, including some quick-turnaround video experimentation

By combining these two different lists, we end up with a list of 106 brands on Twitter, as seen in Figure 2.2, which is a great sample to understand how the world's biggest and most innovative brands are using Twitter. I should also mention that a few brands have multiple Twitter accounts, so in each of those cases, I tried my best to choose the account that best represented the brand's social presence.

I should also note that this list is used throughout the book to establish a baseline for how brands use Twitter (this chapter), for Known Events (chapter 3), and Micro-Events (chapter 4), but in chapter 4, I also

Top Brands on Twitter: The 2013 Interbrand 100 + Select RTM Brands

@3Mnews	@Dell	@Intel	@Panasonic
@Accenture	@DennysDiner	@JackDaniels_US	@Pepsi
@Adidas	@DesignByIKEA	@JCPenney	@Philips
@Adobe	@DiGiornoPizza	@JNJCares	@PizzaHut
@Allianz	@Discovery	@JohnDeere	@Porsche
@Amazon	@Disney	@JohnnieWalkerUS	@Prada
@AmericanExpress	@Duracell	@JPMorgan	@RalphLauren
@Arbys	@eBay	@Kelloggs_US	@SamsungMobile
@Audi	@Facebook	@KFC	@SantanderUK
@AvonInsider	@FerrariUSA	@Kia	@SAP
@AXA	@Ford	@Kleenex	@Shell
@Bing	@Gain	@Loreal	@Siemens
@BMWUSA	@Gap	@LouisVuitton	@Smirnoff
@Budweiser	@Generalelectric	@Mastercard	@Sony
@Burberry	@Gillette	@MBUSA	@Sprite
@Butterfinger	@GoldmanSachs	@McDonalds	@Starbucks
@CanonUSAimaging	@GoogleNexus	@MoetUSA	@ThomsonReuters
@Cartier	@Gucci	@MorganStanley	@Tide
@Caterpillarinc	@HarleyDavidson	@MTV	@TiffanyAndCo
@Charmin	@Heineken	@Nescafe	@Toyota
@Chevrolet	@HJHeinzCompany	@Nike	@UPS
@Cisco	@HM	@NintendoAmerica	@Visa
@Citi	@Honda	@NissanUSA	@VW
@CocaCola	@HP	@Nokia	@XeroxCorp
@Colgate	@HSBC_UK_press	@Oracle	@Zara
@Corona	@Hyundai	@Oreo	
@Dannon	@IBM	@Pampers	

Figure 2.2   Twitter handles for the 100+ brands in our RTM data set

bring in data from additional brands to round out the data set. With micro-trends, that's just what we have to do to get a good sample of brand content.

We've got a solid list, but now we need some data. Let's go get it.

THE DATA SET

How should we analyze all these different accounts? I suppose we could just check out the last few Tweets from each brand, manually, and try to put together some insights around each. Or we could just pick the top content that has made headlines and leave it at that. But we're better than that, right?

There's a ton of data out there for us to collect, segment, and analyze, so let's build out a database full of social goodness. Here's how we'll do it:

1) First, create a Twitter list for these 106 brands (you can see the one I built at https://twitter.com/chriskerns/lists/trendology).
2) Then write some code to ask Twitter for the last 3,200 Tweets (the limit that the Twitter Public API will currently return) from each brand on this list. Some of the brands had fewer than 3,200 tweets, and if that was the case, I just asked the API for every Tweet created by the brand since they started their social efforts.
3) For each Tweet, we will store all the information that will help us learn about the social behavior of our brands in a local database. The data includes:
   - the full text of each Tweet, including hashtags and links
   - the brand screen name that wrote each Tweet
   - how many followers each brand has
   - the date/time of when each Tweet was created
   - the number of retweets each Tweet received
   - the number of favorites each Tweet received

By walking through these steps, we end up with over 260,000 brand Tweets from the past few years that received, in total, over 18,500,000 retweets and about 5,000,000 favorites from Twitter users.

Remember, this entire data set was created using tools and data that are available to the general public. I didn't use any proprietary access to social data, or a set of fancy analytics tools. I manually gathered a list of brands I was interested in and used Python code to ping the Twitter public API. Said a different way: *you can do this at home.*

We'll use this data to look at what brands Tweet, how they Tweet, when they Tweet, what they include in their Tweets, and more. And most importantly, we'll take a good look at how each of these tactics performs, and which social strategies are getting the biggest reaction from their social audience. But first, we need to understand how to measure success.

REAL-TIME SUCCESS DEFINITION

When you get a huge amount of data, the first instinct is to jump right in and start pulling numbers. But let's step back for a minute and understand what we'll be measuring in this book, and more importantly why we'll define success in certain ways. Success measurement is no cake walk, especially in social media across 100+ brands, so we should make sure we're on the same page before moving ahead.

What follows is a breakdown of some common key performance indicators (KPIs) used to measure the success of social media and, more specifically, real-time marketing. A few caveats before we continue:

This RTM Dataset Is Twitter Based

Because our data set is built from Twitter data, we'll limit our measurement discussion to Twitter success metrics. Also know that Facebook is making a case for continuing to increase its share of real-time conversation, and other social networks, such as Pinterest and Instagram, could be used under certain circumstances for RTM. And new platforms can always emerge as RTM candidates in the future, such as messaging upstarts SnapChat and WhatsApp, which don't currently have a huge brand presence or infrastructure, but probably will at some point.

Social Media Measurement Is a Big Topic

This is by no means a book that covers every aspect of social media measurement. This is more of a primer to get us started in how to measure success for social, but specifically for real-time marketing.

Let's start with a few high-level goals that we can frame our success measurement around, and we'll begin with the biggest, most debated one on the list: engagement.

ENGAGEMENT

Engagement, the measurement of audience interaction with a brand's content, gets a bad rap from a lot of people. It's not directly tied to revenue, they say. It doesn't mean anything, they cry. But I think those people are wrong.

Getting the audience to interact with something you've created as a brand is a pretty amazing thing. It shows that what you created actually interests an individual, and it indicates that the audience feels some sort of connection with your brand. It shows that the content you send out resonates with the audience and that they are on your side. It's the new soft sell, and brands all over the world are engaging their audience every day via social media. In fact, I'd go as far to say that if a brand doesn't believe that engaging their customers is an important part of business in today's world, they probably don't belong on social media in the first place.

It's silly to think that revenue, and not engagement, is the only value measurement that matters to a brand in today's social world. If you're looking to increase revenue via social media, that's great. In fact, that's amazing. Add that goal to your KPIs, and create campaigns and social media efforts to get that revenue. You can build targeted social efforts that play off the best parts of each channel, and entice your followers with a specific offer than be traced back to that social experience. I see clients do it every day—and it makes them a lot of money. But that doesn't mean that increasing your touchpoints with your audience isn't worth a lot to your brand as well.

Jim Sterne, who wrote the book *Social Media Metrics*, knows all about the perception issues that engagement has received as a success metric in social media. "It's a perfectly wonderful measurement," Sterne argues, "but everyone wants it to be something absolutely specific, and it's not. I always love to equate marketing with dating, and if you can get someone engaged in conversation that's great, it's a start. But at different points in the relationship, engagement means different things. I've been married for thirty-seven years and engagement means something very different to me now than when I was trying to get someone to go to the prom with me." The main problem with some marketers' not trusting engagement is that it truly does mean different things to different organizations, but that's not necessarily a bad thing. Sterne continues, "So as long as we back off of engagement having to be a specific formula or a specific number, then it's a good thing for a brand to strive for. The measurement is different depending on where you are in the cycle and what you're trying to accomplish."[2]

Engagement is a great way to begin the conversation with an audience, and many brands want to use social media to do exactly that. Many brands employ a social strategy that focuses on building their brand first and holding off on a sales pitch until later in the relationship. In fact, many brands don't want to sell you something with every Facebook post or every Instagram photo. They want people that follow their brand to understand the ins and outs of the brand—their offerings, their opinions, their voice. They want to blend into your social stream without sticking out too much—remember the weird guy at the party trying to sell you something? They want to avoid being that guy every day. By working their way into your daily routine, they can slip in offers now and then without coming on too strong. These are offers that you might even share with others with the click of a button, because now you trust that brand.

While it's possible to monetize engagement, I'm not going to dive into details around that in this book. Many companies assign dollar values to different levels of engagement, and while I support that practice, that belongs in a different book. Assigning value is a very customized process, and coming up with a dollar value across 100+ brands will be misleading at best. Trying to measure the exact dollar value of engagement, with any accuracy, is a bit like trying to figure out how this morning's three-mile run impacted your life expectancy, in hours. You could come up with a number, but it would probably be wrong and just used as encouragement to keep you from hitting the snooze button. You don't need a number. You know that running this morning has helped you be healthier and feel better about yourself, so you lace up your running shoes and get out there. Each individual morning run doesn't need to be quantified—and this is coming from an analytics guy.

ENGAGEMENT—HOW DO WE MEASURE IT?

Favorites—Favorites are the equivalent of a "Like" button on Twitter, where the audience shows you their support for a Tweet without sharing it out to their network. To favorite something, users can click on the star icon that is visible in the Twitter interface underneath every Tweet. It's easy to see how many favorites any Tweet has by clicking through to the Tweet detail view where the metrics are visible.

Replies—Another measure of how audiences are engaging with your Twitter content is through the number of replies you receive. Users can reply by hitting the "reply" button and sending you a note back to tell you what they think, how much they like you, or what an idiot you are. Replies are tougher to measure, however, because Twitter no longer returns the number of replies per tweet in its API. If you want to count these, you can do so with the help of an social analytics toolset. Fortunately there are tons available on the market today.

SHARING THE LOVE

Getting the audience to share a social media post is an amazing feeling. It means the content not only connected with your customer but was funny/good/insightful enough for them to attach it to their own personal brand. When a brand does the hard work of crafting a unique voice with something interesting to say (read: not an ad), you'll up your chances of getting that content passed around and shared. And shares don't only count in the shares bucket, they also increase impressions and have a real impact on followers.

Social audiences share brand content frequently, and this action gives brands the perfect opportunity to capitalize on the channel's norms to get their message in front of more eyeballs. Twitter's design makes sharing easy and painless for users and has created an environment in which sharing is a common activity. These factors make social media channels pretty unique as far as marketing environments go. Let me put it this way—how many times have you read an email from a brand

and immediately shared it with everyone on your contact list? Yeah, exactly. My number is zero, too.

SHARING—HOW DO WE MEASURE IT?

Retweets (RTs)—The retweet is the primary metric for measuring sharing activity on Twitter. With a simple click of the "retweet" icon, you send the Tweet you're reading into the Twitter streams of all your followers.

Modified Tweets (MTs)—The MT is my favorite off-the-books measurement for Twitter sharing. You see, there's no true functionality in the platform to create a MT, people have just done it on their own. You copy the Tweet that someone sent, including their username, add some commentary of your own, and label it as a "modified Tweet." They get credit, and you continue the conversation. It's a form of social sharing that's off the books, but you should be counting it.

Campaign Hashtag Mentions—To spread the word, you don't need to have followers retweet exactly what you said. If you're using a unique hashtag or phrase in your campaign, you can track usage of that to show how far the word is spreading. In many cases, organic uses of your branded hashtag are even better than having someone simply hit "Retweet"—it can be a huge boost to your brand to have an influencer support your campaign in their own words and social content.

AUDIENCE

Followers are the number of people actively receiving your social content on Twitter. These are individual users who have chosen to receive your social posts in their news feed, and this number indicates that what a brand is talking about is resonating with the audience. Traditionally, follower count has been a nice big vanity metric that lets a brand compare how it's doing to the competition in an apples-to-apples manner, but smart social media teams have learned that this metric isn't just about bragging rights anymore. Increasing a brand's follower count is about creating a valuable social asset that earns the company greater reach with future efforts. Also, let's not forget an important fact: people can also unfollow your brand. Building a follower base shows that you're not only building new connections but also retaining your existing ones with every piece of content you post.

AUDIENCE—HOW DO WE MEASURE IT?

Followers—Every time these users bring up Twitter in a browser or in a mobile app, they have the chance of seeing your most recent Tweet. Twitter doesn't currently throttle the views of organic posts—meaning that for every Tweet a brand posts, their followers will see it if they are on the network around the same time period.

REACH

Reach is a metric that hasn't been shared for organic Tweets to date, but I'm hoping this changes in the near future. Understanding how many people actually saw your post or Tweet will allow brands to understand not only raw counts of actions (engagement, shares, etc.) but also the rate at which that action is happening based on the number of views a piece of content received. For example, if 100 people share my Tweet, that's interesting to know, but doesn't tell me the whole story. On the other hand, if I know that 100 people shared my tweet out of the 1,000 people who actually saw it, that's an amazing share rate of 10 percent. With access to impression data, I can then measure the success of different campaigns in an apples-to-apples method.

REACH—HOW DO WE MEASURE IT?

For now, what we have is a calculation of "potential impressions," which is a bit of a ballpark number. It goes a little something like this:

Twitter Potential Impression Metric: Followers X Posts—For every post you make, each of your followers has the potential of seeing it at least once. How many actually see it? Only Twitter knows that—for now.

OTHER METRICS
Depending on the type of real-time marketing campaign you're considering and what you're looking to directly impact, there are a few more buckets of KPIs that you'll want to consider. Here are just a few of them:

REVENUE

Yes, I can hear you saying, everything a company does should lead to revenue. Why aren't we using that as a measurement for success here? Well, we can measure return on investment (ROI) for brands on social media, but it's going to look different for every industry and every social strategy that each brand uses. That's just the nature of social media. Outside of this book I've built plenty of case studies for individual brands, showing how a revenue-based campaign has created great ROI via social, but the plain truth is that it's difficult to do across 100+ brands due to the diversity of tactics and lack of available public data.

In this book, we'll focus on measuring success across a wide variety of the world's top brands with data that is available across the entire set, and engagement and sharing metrics best fit that bill. Brands will want to take advantage of what they learn from this book to translate RTM success over to their revenue-generating campaigns, but to measure an industry-wide revenue impact is beyond the scope of what we're going for in this study. Engagement, sharing, and follower measurements are used to gauge social media success across the industry, and they'll be our metrics for RTM success as well.

SIGN-UPS

If your campaign includes some kind of conversion event (offer redemption, sweepstakes, etc.) you'll obviously want to include those metrics in your KPIs. And with all conversion events, you don't just want a raw number of people who signed up to win your new truck or registered for your white paper. You'll want to know the funnel metrics for that event as well. How many people saw it -> how many people clicked -> how many people actually filled out the form -> how many people completed the process. Again, this is a difficult thing to measure across 100+ brands, so we won't be using it as an industry-wide success measurement in this study, but it's absolutely relevant for measuring success of a single campaign.

BRAND MENTIONS

This is a simple mention of your @username in a tweet by someone other than your brand on Twitter. Growth in this metric indicates that the conversation about your brand is growing, but you'll want to support that metric with an understanding of sentiment as well. More mentions of your brand that are angry or negative shouldn't be counted toward your measures of success.

PRESS MENTIONS

Sometimes brands participate in RTM with one of the goals (not the *only* goal, but *one* of the goals) to be possibly mentioned in the trades the next day. And don't lie. A mention of "winning the social Super Bowl" in *Ad Age* isn't exactly a sharp stick in the eye for any marketer. It's worth at least a week's worth of press mentions, and another cycle during the next big event covering what you'll be up to in order to defend your real-time marketing crown. But I will say this, if the only reason you're doing RTM is to try and get some press, you should rethink your strategy. It's a nice side benefit, but if there's one thing this book was designed to do, it's to convince you that there's real data to support why your social team should engage in real-time marketing beyond just betting on your own Oreo moment.

HOW DO BRANDS USE TWITTER?

So we've got some success metrics and a whole bunch of data. Now it's time to put it to use. Let's analyze the data from a few different angles and take a couple of quick looks at how brands use Twitter day to day. Which brands are primarily using Twitter as a one-on-one communication platform? Which brands are getting the most out of their hashtags? How does overall Twitter behavior break out across all of our 100+ brands?

TWITTER COMMUNICATION TACTICS

The first thing we'll want to do is understand the different types of Twitter content the network supports, and how brands are using each approach. There are many different tactics that a brand or media company can use on a social network—broadcasting messages to the masses, echoing the messages of others, and replying directly to users. How often are companies using each method to balance their social strategy?

Here's a breakdown of our content-type buckets on Twitter.

1: ORIGINAL CONTENT

Original content created by brands and media companies on Twitter includes all messages that are meant for the masses and are generated

Figure 2.3   Original Twitter content from the @Pampers Twitter account

Figure 2.4 A reply from the @Pizzahut Twitter account

exclusively by the company. Original content on Twitter can include posts about product news, questions for followers to answer, or a call to action for the user to find out more about a topic.

2: REPLIES

Many brands use Twitter as a valuable customer service channel. Using the reply functionality, brands can talk one-on-one with customers to address concerns, to communicate back to a customer who has reached out with a question or comment, or sometimes just to reach out and say hi. All of those conversations can be seen if you visit the brand's Twitter page, but won't show up in your feed unless you follow both the brand and the individual that is being replied to.

3: RETWEETS

Retweets by brands echo the remarks of other people or companies, and are sent out to their followers by simply clicking the "Retweet" button instead of crafting original content. By sharing the content of others, the brand is associating itself with the original Twitter user as well as the message being retweeted.

So now that we've defined our three buckets, let's look at how often the world's most valuable brands are using each tactic (Figure 2.6).

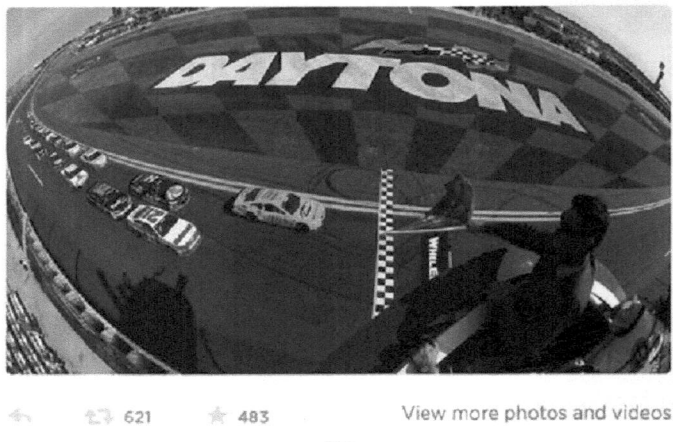

Figure 2.5   A Tweet from the @NASCAR Twitter account, retweeted by 3M

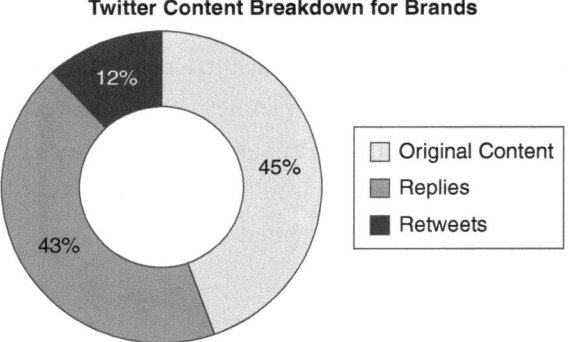

Figure 2.6   Twitter content tactics by the 100+ brands in this study, based on their most recent 260,000+ Tweets

The top brands in the world are using Twitter for a mass-communication device (posting Tweets to all followers) in roughly equal proportion to one-to-one communication with customers and other Twitter users. Retweets make up a smaller portion (12%) of overall Tweets. From a high level, brands are mostly on Twitter to share original content and reach out to their audience one-on-one.

When we dive into the real-time marketing performance study in the next chapter, we're going to ignore retweets and replies and focus on the original brand content, but let's explore this data while we're here and see what we can learn.

We'll start with replies—the Twitter functionality that transforms your brand's megaphone into a nice, hand-written thank-you note. Isn't that nice, your Mom says.

COME @ ME

With replies making up 43 percent of the Twitter brand content in our data set, we'll want to understand more about this popular practice. Replies are a great way for brands to reach out to individual customers and have a conversation without sending that message out to the company's entire follower base. Replies are used to communicate back to individuals who have mentioned your brand with many different use cases. If someone gives your brand a shout-out saying how much they love your burritos, your social media team can ping back a simple "thank you" and hopefully make that customer's day. When customers ask about product details or experience service issues, replies can speedily provide answers or direct the user to the right channel to resolve their issue. It's a great tactic to make a customer feel like the brand is hearing their message and acknowledging their presence.

Replies aren't designed to get a brand huge reach or engage a large audience. They are meant for a smaller set of eyes, and the engagement numbers in our data set shows tells that story. Brand replies from our data set received an average 1.12 retweets and 1.76 favorites from followers, which is much, much lower than original content. How much lower? We'll find out in a few pages, but it makes sense that if the Tweets are only being seen by a few individuals, there will be less chance for engagement.

Figure 2.7   A Twitter conversation between @USAirways and yours truly

Figure 2.7 shows an example of a reply from my own Twitter account and an exchange with a company's social media team. While the US Airways social media team couldn't fix my tray table, their response had an interesting impact on my journey. When I saw a duct-taped tray table as I sat down, two things immediately came to mind:

1) "Great, I can't use my tray table" and
2) "Oh my God where else is there duct tape on this plane?"

I was irritated, and Tweeted out the picture to help release some of my frustration. Getting a reply back before the plane even took off (just five minutes later) actually did ease my mind, and while I knew the social media team couldn't come in and fix the problem, the fact that they were acknowledging the issue and had processes in place to listen to social customer complaints was an indicator that maybe question #2 wasn't really a problem. Maybe the duct tape fix was just an anomaly and not a sign of chronic problems with the company. My tray table didn't get fixed, but the Twitter interaction did help improve my perception of the US Airways brand.

So who are the brands leveraging replies to help their business? Is this persistent across all brands, or are there super-repliers that are skewing the numbers? As you would expect, there are brands at both extremes, both using replies as the majority of their Twitter communication and hardly ever using the practice.

The most active brands from our data set that are using replies on Twitter are

- Pizza Hut (99% of content)
- Visa (98% of content)
- Oreo (98% of content)
- Coca-Cola (97% of content)
- Nike (92% of content)
- Arby's (90% of content)

Feeling lonely? Don't worry—Pizza Hut is here to reach out and talk to you one-on-one. That's right, Pizza Hut is the main reply aficionado versus the other brands in this study, and they reach out to consumers *a lot*. From the last 3,000 Pizza Hut Tweets I looked at, 2,992 were replies directly at Twitter users.

On the other side, some brands include hardly any replies in their social strategies. Louis Vuitton, Accenture, Zara, and Morgan Stanley have hardly any (less than 1%) of their content being sent with replies. The absence of replies doesn't mean their social media teams are lacking in any level of sophistication. It just means that they have chosen not to use Twitter for this type of communication.

So what's the takeaway here? If your brand isn't currently using replies as a tactic to give some one-on-one love to your audience, you should consider it as part of your social media plan. Even if you don't use the practice in your personal Twitter use, you should know it's a huge tool for some of the biggest brands in the world to reach out and make a personal connection with their followers.

Now let's move our lens to the smallest content group from our first analysis: retweets.

SAY "SOCIAL SHARING" TEN TIMES FAST

The retweet is everyone's favorite way to share on Twitter: the retweet. In essence, it's a tactic that takes content that someone else (or another brand) posted, and proclaims support for the message through sharing, whether it's a cause, a joke, or whatever else lies within that Tweet. With a click of a "Retweet" button, brands can support a message and tie themselves to another brand by doing so. So which brands are doing this with a high degree of frequency?

The most active brands using retweets on Twitter are

- Siemens (60% of content)
- 3MNews (49% of content)
- HSBC (38% of content)
- Sony (38% of content)
- IBM (36% of content)

Siemens is leading the brands in our data set in this category (60% of their Twitter feeds are made up of retweets), followed by 3M and HSBC. It's no mistake that this list is made up of a good number of brands that use their Twitter channel to distribute news and other industry information to their followers. Retweeting is a good practice when there's frequent news about an industry or vertical that a brand would like to share, especially in a business-to-business environment. It would be tough to imagine Swiss Miss retweeting a press release to its followers about chocolate futures due to an upcoming drought, but it might make sense for the parent brand, ConAgra, to do just that.

If that theory is correct, then our data should tell us that consumer brands aren't retweeting that much, right? The data agrees. Consumer-facing brands like Pizza Hut and Prada are tied for the lowest RT percent with zero, zilch, nada RTs in their last 3,200 Tweets. They are joined by other consumer brands, like Oreo, Visa, and IKEA, all of which leave retweeting mostly out of their social media playbooks, with under 1 percent of their content made up of retweets. These brands like to create their own original content and leave the sharing to other brands.

While we're on the subject, who, exactly, are these brands sharing content from? Well, that's going to differ by brand, but the most retweeted accounts by the top 100 brands are actually the brands themselves. Yes, many brands have multiple Twitter accounts for different subbrands or corporate functions, and the data shows that a majority of the retweet activity by brands is actually retweets of content from their sister accounts. So @AvonInsider retweets @AvonPRGals in high frequency, @HSBC_UK_press retweets @HSBC_press, the @Sony account retweets @SonyElectronics and @Playstation. And why not, right? Followers won't mind if the content is still relevant to them, and the brand gets a boost in the reach of its message.

LET'S TALK PERFORMANCE

It's easy to talk about which brands are doing what, but what we care about as marketers isn't just how often brands use certain practices. We care about how the audience responds to those practices. So we'll take our data crunching to the next level and look at not only what brands are doing but how the followers are engaging with the content. For brand Tweets, the best way for us to measure engagement and sharing is through favorites and retweets. As we dive through this brand study, those are the two main metrics we'll look at to gauge how effective Twitter content has been. There are a few different ways to do this, and we'll walk through each.

ORIGINAL CONTENT PERFORMANCE

Let's start by looking at the original Twitter content from our brands. When we remove all retweets and replies from our data set, we end up with just over 117,000 Tweets that companies have created themselves and intended for their entire audience to see. We'll start at a high level with an understanding that averages across big data sets can be dangerous if taken as gospel, as any good analyst knows that outliers can skew results and lead to false understanding. We won't fall for that trap—we'll start with a 30,000-foot view of brand content performance to simply set a baseline and then dive in deeper to learn what's working and what's not working. Let's start with the simplest measurement approach—overall engagement and sharing patterns.

DIVING INTO RAW ACTION COUNTS

On average across our 106 brands, I'm seeing the average original Tweet receive about 50 retweets and 40 favorites. The median values (retweet median: 7, favorites median: 7) show us that the averages are a bit misleading. The variation of this data is pretty large, which makes sense for many reasons.

- All of our brands have a different number of followers, some dramatically different from others. If a brand gets their message in front of 50,000 followers versus a brand that has 7,000,000 followers, they should see a dramatically different raw number of interactions by the audience
- All Tweets are not the same. Some Tweets are built with different purposes in mind, and therefore receive different levels of engagement and sharing
- The averages are inflated by a few superstar Tweets that have received a huge amount of engagement and sharing

Again, averages can mislead our thinking about what the norm is in social, so let's start digging into the story behind this data. To do this, we'll first look at the distribution of Tweets across our chosen success metrics.

Let's take a quick look at the distribution of our 117,000+ original content brand Tweets by plotting each Tweet's retweet and favorite counts.

On the scatter plot in Figure 2.8, each dot represents a Tweet, and it's positioned via the number of retweets and favorites each piece of brand content received. It gives us a high-level look at how Tweets are distributed with raw counts of engagement. That dot you see in the far right corner is Arby's, waving at you as they try on Pharrell's hat,

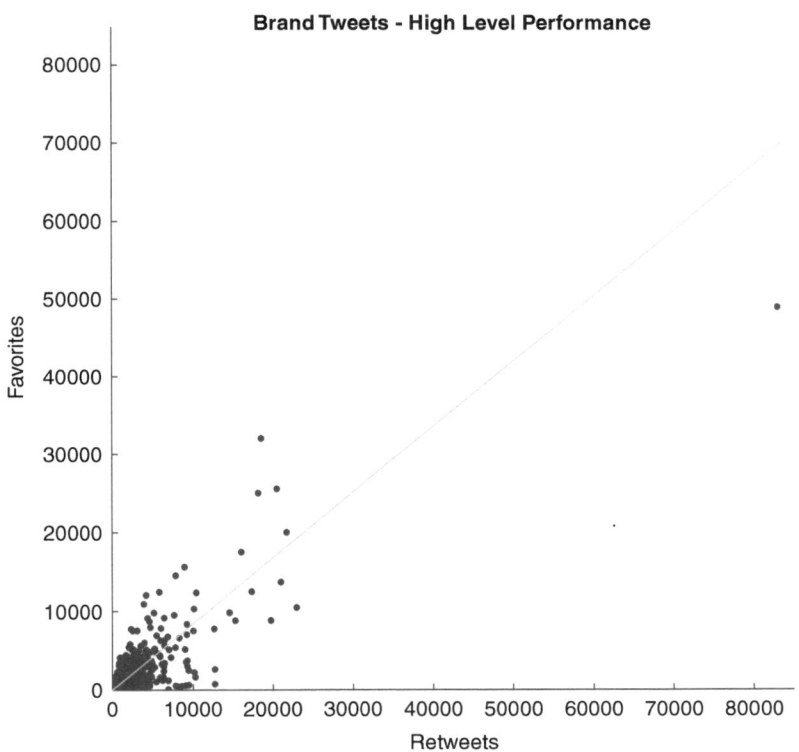

Figure 2.8 A distribution of brand Tweet performance by raw retweet and favorite counts

but there are plenty of other brands that have tweeted content that are receiving a huge amount of engagement and sharing activity from their follower base, including JCPenney, Budweiser, and Starbucks. The majority of this content, however, is down in the bottom left corner with closer-to-earth levels of activity, and closer to our average and median levels.

The trend line tells us that the data points tend to stick to the middle between the two axes. Our two success metrics (retweets and favorites) have a tendency toward the middle of the graph. That is to say, they are somewhat correlated, or when one occurs, the other occurs as well. In fact, when we run a measurement of this (called the correlation coefficient) on these two sets of numbers, they have an 85 percent correlation, which is considered pretty strong. So, for the most part, when a Tweet has content that causes a user to retweet, it's also causing users to favorite.

RATIOS RULE

What we've been talking about so far are raw counts—the exact number of success events each Tweet has received. But as I mentioned, this is going to cause a wide variation in our data set due to many factors, most notably follower count. Let's fix that.

As a practice, brands shouldn't be focusing on raw numbers when it comes to success metrics. Success isn't just getting the largest number of people to retweet your content; rather, you should be aiming for success metrics based on the percent of followers that take some kind of action. If you have 5,000 followers and get 50 of them to favorite one of your Tweets, you can be pretty happy with that level of engagement. On the other hand, if you get 50 favorites from 20M followers, you might want to rethink your strategy.

What do these success metrics look like if we normalize for the number of followers each brand has? To be completely accurate, we would want to measure the number of followers each brand had when each of their Tweets was created, but that data is not possible to obtain from the

Twitter public API. So instead, I grabbed the current level of followers for each of our 100+ brands, and turned each retweet and favorite count into a ratio based on each brand's follower base. We'll use this number as a proxy, knowing it won't be 100 percent accurate.

If we divide each success metric by the number of followers each brand has, some of the top content now includes Tweets from Butterfinger, Gain, Arby's, and DiGiorno. In addition, we're now seeing an even larger tendency for retweets and favorites to co-occur, with a 91 percent correlation coefficient.

Now let's come back full circle and look at our averages. If you'll remember, we said that the average original content brand tweet received 50 RTs and 40 favorites. But what we should be looking at is the ratio of retweets per follower and favorites per follower. So what do those averages look like? The average company receives a retweet from .02 percent of followers and a favorite from .01 percent of every follower. But the average can be misleading, as it is here. When we look at the distribution of performance by brand in Figure 2.9, we see a long tail of reduced performance.

This view differs from the scatter plot in that it only looks at retweets, but is also the average for each brand, instead of showing the performance for each individual Tweet. This view shows that some brands are clearly outperforming others. But what are the brands that are seeing high performance with their retweet and favorite metrics doing more than other brands? Let's keep going and see if we can find out.

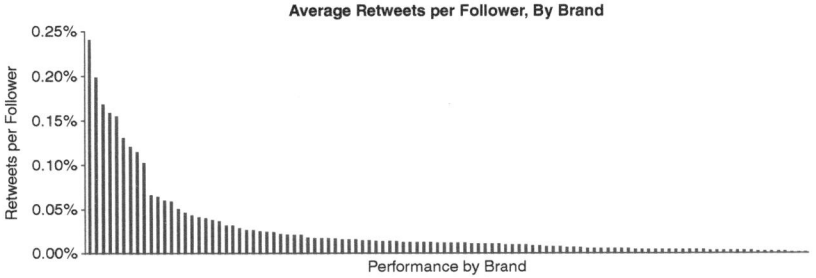

Figure 2.9 Distribution of average retweets per follower across our 100+ brands

PERFORMANCE BY BRAND

Things really start getting interesting when we begin segmenting and looking at different slices of our data set to answer specific questions. Twitter data is great because there are tons of dimensions we can use to segment the data—everything from text to geolocation to time of day. But for now, let's slice by brand (or, in the Twitter world, a data dimension known as "screen name") and see which brands are seeing top performance from a handful of different tactics on Twitter.

We'll start with overall engagement. Which of the top brands in the world are seeing the largest response from their social audience? Who has their social campaigns creating huge levels of engagement and sharing? We'll avoid the temptation of just looking at raw counts and look at our ratios of actions per follower instead. Which brands are not just getting the largest raw number of responses on Twitter but are also speaking to their audience to get the most effective return on their social asset (their follower base)?

We saw a few superstar Tweets that registered high numbers, but Figure 2.10 shows a quick look at which brands are doing the best across the whole of their content.

When we normalize the engagement and sharing by the pool of followers for each brand, and again stack-rank the top brands, we see leaders emerge. Arby's, Budweiser, Visa, and DiGiorno, among others, are getting the best performance out of their Tweets based on the potential number of impressions.

Top Retweets per Follower		Top Favorites per Follower	
Arby's	.24%	Visa	.38%
Budweiser	.20%	Butterfinger	.30%
Butterfinger	.17%	DiGiorno	.17%
Visa	.16%	Budweiser	.16%
DiGiorno	.16%	Arby's	.15%
Johnnie Walker	.13%	Ferrari USA	.12%

Figure 2.10   Top brands on Twitter based on per follower performance ratios

But we shouldn't be satisfied with just knowing the top brands that are doing well on Twitter—we should also probably figure out *why* they are doing well. Let's look at a few patterns that we can see from a few of our top brands:

Visa

The top-performing content for Visa at the time of this analysis resulted from 2014 Sochi Olympics-related conversation. Their use of the #everywhere and #TeamVisa hashtags and mentions of their sponsor athletes (Tracy Gold, Julia Mancuso, and Joannie Rochette, to name a few) received a great response from their audience.

Budweiser

The King of Beers has some interesting tactics in their top 20 Tweets from over the past few years. First and foremost, Budweiser is a big participant in real-time marketing, and sees a great response from their followers when they do so. In addition, Budweiser capitalizes on smaller events to get their follower base motivated. Their campaign to make Major League Baseball's opening day a national holiday (by getting 100,000 signatures on a petition to the White House) received a great response from their followers. They also use hashtags in very smart ways—by jumping on national trends (getting a good response from big event hashtags like #SuperBowl and #WorldSeries) and making their own (#BestBuds, for a puppy that joins their iconic Clydesdale team.)

DiGiorno

My goodness, what can I say about DiGiorno? If you want to talk about a brand that has certainly found its own unique voice on a social channel, you should look to DiGiorno as the poster boy for having fun and finding success while doing it. Similar to Budweiser, six of DiGiorno's top ten Tweets when measured for level of audience response happened during the 2014 Super Bowl. In addition, nine of their top ten included text in ALL CAPS, a technique that has become a recognizable hallmark of the brand in followers' Twitter feeds.

WHEN DO BRANDS TWEET?

Social media is a channel that's open 24 hours a day, and keeping up the appearance of a constant presence can be a huge challenge for brands. With our data set, we can take a look at Tweet patterns across our 100+ brands to see when the most Twitter content is posted. Overall it peaks with working hours, but isn't limited to 9 to 5.

If we look at the schedules for our brands on Twitter in Figure 2.11, they generally start to wake up at around 8 to 9 a.m. EST. Posts peak at noon and then degrade each hour, but are still happening (in small frequency) during nighttime hours. As you can see, the patterns for original posts and replies correlate very closely, so it looks like brands are posting original content and individual replies at roughly the same rate throughout the day. Overall, social media for brands is a full-time job, but it mostly falls within normal working hours.

These views of our data show us when brands are active on Twitter, but the question remains: when *should* brands be posting on Twitter?

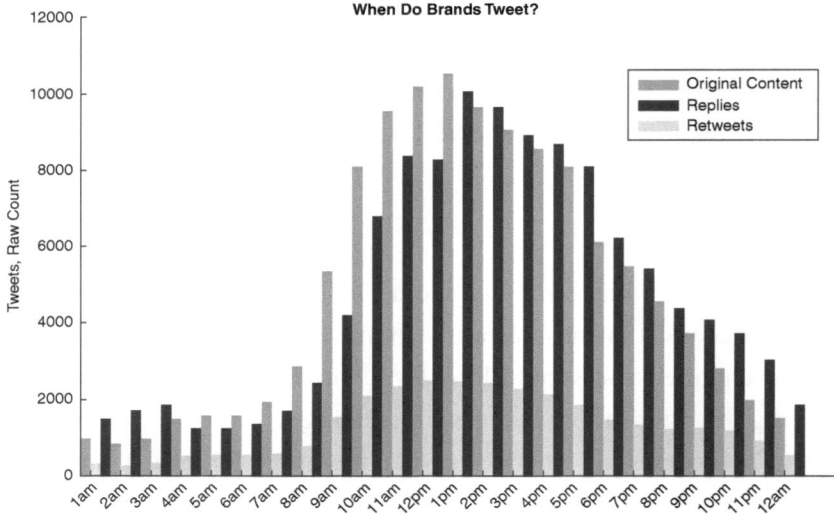

Figure 2.11 Brand Tweets, replies, and retweets by hour (EST)

WHEN ARE AUDIENCES RESPONDING?

Now that we know some patterns around when brands are active on Twitter, let's look at the other side of the equation: when are followers engaging with the content? Do Tweets posted at 9 a.m. get a greater response versus 9 p.m.? Are followers cruising Twitter at lunchtime and ready to favorite or retweet content in higher frequency? Let's look at average effectiveness of Tweets by the hour across our 100+ brands.

If we look at raw counts of engagement, we'll throw off what we're really trying to achieve here. Brands with large follower bases, like Samsung and its seven million plus Twitter followers, will skew our numbers and not give us the true measure we're going for: actions per follower. To combat this, we'll once again want to normalize our data based on followers for each brand. Let's grab the average retweets per follower and favorites per follower by hour and throw those into a graph (Figure 2.12). That should help get rid of these outliers.

Do you see that 6 p.m. spike?! Of course you do. And if we dive into the data, the spike seems legit. The top 20 tweets in this time slot were

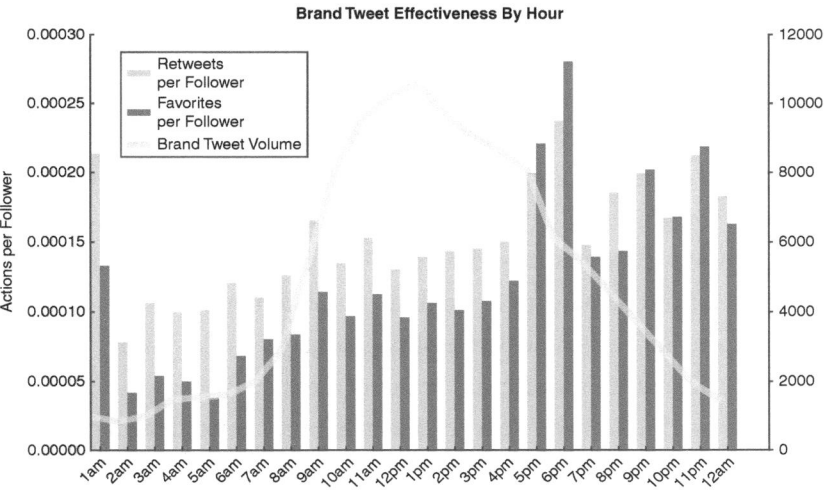

Figure 2.12   Brand Tweet effectiveness by hour, with an overlay of when brands Tweet the most original content

posted by ten different brands, all on different days, all with different types of messaging. And looking again at the graph, we can also see an overall trend that tweet performance steadily rises throughout the day until 1 a.m. EST, and then resets itself at a lower level.

And if you'll notice, I also juxtaposed the performance data with our first view of brand tweets by hour so we can fully appreciate the true takeaway from this data: while brands are mostly observing working hours for their social activity, audience engagement is highly correlated with brand Tweets that are posted in the evening hours. The top right corner of Figure 2.12 identifies a huge opportunity for brands, and it's happening when most social media teams are asleep at the wheel.

Time series are only one aspect of social data that we can examine to gain a better understanding of not only how brands are behaving on Twitter but also what works best to drive engagement with their audience. Let's look at a few more.

HASHTAGS—GENERATING ENGAGEMENT AND SHARING, ONE # AT A TIME

Hashtags, the common way on Twitter to add a trend or category label to your Tweets, are commonly referred to as a best practice for both individual users and brands alike. Hashtags help keep a common thread going in a conversation, and also allow brands to jump in on a trend that is happening in other circles. Hashtags are frequently used by brands in original content—in fact, looking at our nice, big collection of brand Tweets, I see hashtags used in 27 percent of @replies, 61 percent of retweets, and 63 percent of original Tweet content.

But does our data show that hashtags actually work to move the needle on performance for original brand content?

When we look at the data for hashtags versus nonhashtag performance in Figure 2.13, and normalize for actions per follower, the case for hashtags in Tweets holds up well. The correlations point to the effectiveness of hashtags—a 46 percent higher retweet rate and 70 percent higher favorite rate with a hashtag versus no hashtag.

	#Hashtag in Tweet	No #Hashtag in Tweet	
Retweets per Follower	0.019%	0.013%	**+46%**
Favorites per Follower	0.017%	0.010%	**+70%**

Figure 2.13   High-level hashtag performance in brand Tweets

But remember, averages can lead us down the wrong path. To make sure that none of our 100+ brands are skewing our results, I also ran individual results for each brand. It turns out that the majority of brands (64 out of 106) are seeing positive results from hashtags versus nonhashtags. Arby's, Butterfinger, and Visa are seeing the biggest performance bumps for their hashtag content.

PUNCTUATION

Twitter famously gives users 140 characters to create a message, and even with such limited space, marketers still have a lot of choices to make as they craft their brand posts for the social world to see. Let's take a quick look at a few different tactics that companies use in Tweets and check the effectiveness of each on Twitter engagement and share rates.

QUESTION MARKS

Think that including a question in your brand Tweet will spark a response from your audience? What better way to get a response than to pose a question to your followers? But does it actually work? Are you noticing all the question marks in this paragraph?

As we can see in Figure 2.14, brands use the practice a fair amount— 17 percent of the original brand tweets, 10 percent of retweets, and 12 percent of @replies I analyzed included a question mark. So how about the performance numbers?

A few brands have had luck with Tweet content that includes questions, including VW (as seen in Figure 2.15), which saw a 7,400 percent+

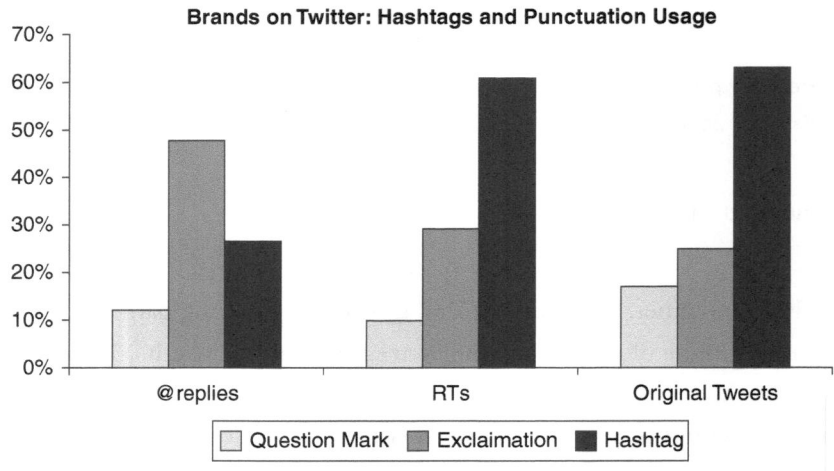

Figure 2.14 Hashtag and punctuation usage in Twitter content by our 100+ brands

Figure 2.15 A Tweet from @VW that asked their followers a question and received great engagement in return

bump in retweets per follower and 5,700 percent+ bump in favorites per follower by asking their followers, "What would you do to drive the Design Vision #VWGTI for a day?" But overall, the practice correlates with 29 percent fewer retweets per follower and 34 percent fewer favorites per follower than tweets without question marks.

EXCLAMATION POINTS!

While not appropriate for all brand voices, exclamation points can help bring a little spice and fun to the copy for the right brands. Twenty-three percent of the original content brand Tweets I looked at included an exclamation point, with 29 percent of retweets and 48 percent of @replies doing the same. Which! Seems! Really! High! But do they perform?

Not on average. The excitable Tweets correlate with 38 percent lower retweets and 44 percent lower favorites than Tweets without an exclamation point. This may be a practice that works for certain companies whose brand voice doesn't mind showing some excitement, but if you're considering adding some ! to your brand that otherwise stays away from the practice, the high-level data doesn't support the argument.

LITTLE SMILEY FACES. SERIOUSLY

While we're on the subject of punctuation, let's get to the good stuff. I'm talking, of course, about brands' usage of smiley faces and wink faces in Tweets.

So, regrettable as it may be, making :-) faces in messages is a thing, even for brands. The ability for brands to convey happiness, a whimsical nature, or whatever other reason a social media manager might have for including these expressions in Tweets is still a relevant topic, mostly because the data supports that they are being used in somewhat mainstream volumes.

It would stand to reason that using these emoticons in replies might make the most sense. It's a personal touch for a brand in a one-on-one communication and, let's face it, a reply will reduce the number of people who see you use these atrocious things, so you can show your face

:-) Emoticons per Reply		;-) Emoticons per Reply	
Nokia	50%	Nokia	14%
Honda	31%	Starbucks	10%
Starbucks	26%	Pepsi	8%
Arby's	19%	Coca-Cola	5%
Coca-Cola	17%	NissanUSA	5%

Figure 2.16　Brands using emoticons in Twitter replies

at work the next day. The data backs this up: across our 100+ brands, I'm seeing that almost 9 percent of reply Tweets include a smiley face or wink emoticon. But the brands doing this with the highest frequency might surprise you (Figure 2.16).

The good news is that I'm pretty sure I'm the only human being in the history of social media who ever ran that analysis. But as silly as it sounds, even the strangest things can tell us a bit about the brands we're looking at and how they work with social media.

When we look at the original Tweet content for each brand, the smiley face and the wink face usage numbers plummet. Smiley faces were only used in 0.7 percent of original content Tweets analyzed from our 100+ brands, and about half that number were bold enough to send a wink face to their entire follower base. Are they making the right call to keep their :-) to one-on-one interaction? Turns out they are. As far as effectiveness goes, original content Tweets with smiley faces receive 46 percent fewer retweets and 36 percent fewer favorites than content without the emoticons. So if you're keeping your emoticons in check, keep doing what you're doing. :-)

THE LANGUAGE OF BRAND TWEETS

Grabbing social data from over 100 brands not only gives us a lot of Tweets, it also gives us a whole lot of text to look through. Each Tweet can contain up to 140 characters, and we can find interesting patterns in how brands communicate with their audience by looking at not only individual brand patterns but also language patterns from our entire data set. Do brands creating original content for Twitter use certain words in high frequency, more than you or I might use? Do brands use predictable patterns of language when communicating one-on-one via Twitter replies with customers? And, most importantly, which of these tactics is proving to be the most effective for brands? With so much data, we'll need to leverage some tools to help give us a 30,000-foot view.

Luckily, help is here via a text analysis technology called natural language processing (NLP), which is built specifically to find patterns in large amounts of language. NLP does a good job of getting a bunch of text together, removing the words you don't care about (boring little words like "I," "me," "our," "at," etc.), and then looking for patterns in how language is used in aggregate.

By using NLP tactics, we can start to understand what brands are talking about with consumers in different situations. Since we've got a boatload of Tweets, we should be able to find some interesting and informative patterns in brand conversations on Twitter.

MOST COMMON TERMS IN BRAND TWITTER REPLIES

What are brands talking about when they use replies to ping individuals? Well, it's difficult to summarize over 115,000 conversations in a few sentences, but we can use some tricks of the trade to get a hint at what's going on.

Here's a list of the most frequently used words that brands use when replying directly to followers in a one-on-one social situation:

- **"thanks"** (ex: "thanks for the love Beth!")
- **"get"** (ex: "Celebrate! You get a $5 @Arbys gift card for joining the #cravewave")
- **"help"** (ex: "Please call our customer service hotline, we have reps that can help")
- **"hear"** (ex: "So sorry to hear that. If you can direct message me lets see if we can take care of that")

- **"please"** (ex: "I'm so sorry to hear this. Can you please send us a DM with details?")
- **"like"** (ex: "Glad you like it!")
- **"love"** (ex: "Thanks for the love!")

As you could probably guess, our most frequent reply terms match language used heavily in customer service scenarios. "Thanks" and "please" come up a lot, which makes perfect sense for a brand that is in customer service mode. "Get" is an indicator of a good number of offers that go out on a one-on-one basis, and is sometimes used by brands in response to a comment about a brand or a customer service issue the Twitter user has been experiencing. "Help" indicates that a lot of brands are either redirecting questions to other customer service avenues or closing the conversation with a "I'm glad we could help" send-off.

MOST COMMON TERMS IN ORIGINAL TWEETS

Let's keep our focus on text analysis, but shift our spotlight to original brand content on Twitter. This is one that should result in some fairly diverse results—mining frequently used language for one brand would be one thing, but mining it across 100+ should give us a big grab bag of terms and phrases used across different verticals and lines of business.

Still, I bet we can learn something by checking out the most frequently used language by our brands and media companies, and natural language processesing will help us do this without having to look through more than 100,000 Tweets one at a time.

Here's a list of some of the most frequently used terms by brands in original Twitter content:

- **"new"** (ex: "Introducing our new special menu. Build your own pancakes!")
- **"today"** (ex: "Good luck to all the nominees today!")
- **"check"** (ex: "Check out videos of #laserlight technology")
- **"like"** (ex: "Now time for something more exciting...like a late night run to McDonald's")

- **"day"** (ex: "Edwin Armstrong, the inventor of FM radio transmission, was born on this day in 1890")
- **"win"** (ex: "We have our winners for #WhatDidIFindInTheWash #LuckOfTheTide style. Answer: Shamrock Headband. Keep following for more fun games to come")

So, when analyzed in aggregate, brand tweets commonly talk about new offerings and what followers can take advantage of "today," ask people to check out something, offer up facts about the day, offer ways to win prizes, and address many, many more topics. On the subject of winning things, if we dive into multiterm phrases and frequency, we see that some of the most frequent occurrences have to do with winning. Phrases like "a chance to win " and "to win a" are in the top ten. And multiterm phrases like "Check out the" and "Check out our" occur in many brand Tweets as well.

WORD IS BOND: AUDIENCE RESPONSE TO LANGUAGE

We now know which terms are being used the most by brands in Tweets, but, as you should be getting used to, we can do better than that. Counting terms and phrases, even if it's with super-cool natural language processing software, doesn't get us the answer we're really looking for. What we really care about is performance, right? So what are the most frequent words and phrases used in successful brand Tweets?

To figure this out, we'll just segment our data set to only include high-performing Tweets. That is to say, Tweets that received more than the average retweets per follower or favorites per follower. Doing this takes us from 117,000+ Tweets to just about 50,000 Tweets, but that's still plenty of content.

In addition, we'll push the functionality of our natural language processing software a bit to find the most effective phrases instead of terms. Phrases (in this case, three-word phrases or "tri-grams") can paint a much better picture of why certain words are resonating, and help all of us marketers learn from the effective tactics others are using.

When we start looking at the multiword phrases, some interesting social tactics used by brands emerge. And because we've segmented our data set to only include high-performing content, we know these tactics are working.

Here's the list of the most effective phrases.

Highly Effective Phrases:

- "photo of the day"
- "a chance to win"
- "check out the"
- "did you know"
- "we hope you"
- "retweet if you"

After checking the top results here, I can see at least a few different tactics we can learn from here. "Photo of the day," which is used mostly by Harley Davidson and receives a great response from their audience, is a daily way to reach out to their follower base with media and align the images with campaigns that are currently top of mind for the brand. "A chance to win" should be obvious—people like to win stuff. But other social calls to action around learning something new, like "check out the" and "did you know" are also returning great engagement and sharing results for brands. Lastly, the phrase "retweet if you" is not only the clearest, simplest call to action on this list, but it turns out that outright asking your audience for retweets actually works.

BRANDS USING TWITTER TRENDS

The speed at which information flows today brings with it trends and headlines that change faster than ever. The ability to access, digest, and share content results in patterns of trending topics that ebb and flow throughout the day and never seem to be the same as the day before.

There's no better example of this than Twitter's Trending Topics feature. Trending Topics appeared on the Twitter home page in 2010 as a way for users to understand the hottest topics across the entire user base and gain visibility on what was being discussed in high frequency. Today, Trending Topics are much more sophisticated than the original, simple list.

Today, Twitter's Trending Topics are assigned in over 300 geographies across the globe, most of which are at the city level but also aggregate up to country and "Worldwide" trends. With this system, Trending Topics can make local topics visible as well as larger trends to give great visibility on real-time topics that will resonate for every location. Here in Austin, Texas, I might see a few Trending Topics about BBQ, while a user at the same time in Chicago is seeing Topics that cover the Cubs having another losing season, but we'll both see a few of the same trends set at the United States and the worldwide level.

These Trending Topics don't only change by geography. They are also updating every minute if a new trend has the velocity to overtake one of the current topics on the list.

For example, let's look at the Trending Topics for a typical Friday—January 24, 2014.

Top Twitter Trends, January 24, 2014:

- #WeWillAlwaysSupportYouJustin
- Kobe
- Justin Bieber
- DUI
- #RejectedGrammyCategories

As Twitter's Trending Topics show us, there were a few things happening that day. Justin Bieber had been arrested for an alleged DUI, Kobe Bryant was announced as a starter for the NBA's All-Star Game, and there was a Twitter meme where users were chiming in with funny rejected categories for the Grammys. But there's also a long tail of trends that occurred throughout the United States, 903 separate trends in total on that Friday, most of which were not visible to the entire country.

If we dive into one of those trends, we can see that the audience across different geographies discussed the topic with different levels of interest. "Yankee Stadium" trended in New York, but nowhere else, for

a total of 35 minutes. "Wendy Davis" trended in Austin for 15 minutes, and "#CouplesTherapy" trended for a few minutes in Arizona,
Louisiana, Nebraska, and Florida. I don't even want to find out what's
going on with that last one, but if you'd like to investigate, please be my
guest and shoot me an email.

So how many of our 100+ brands have used hashtags and phrases
that are on the Twitter Trending Topic list? We're going to find out, but
we're also going to answer the question we really want to know: "Is this
working for them?" We're getting to that. I know, I know—I'm such a
tease.

A HIGH-LEVEL LOOK AT TRENDING TOPIC PERFORMANCE

To analyze the performance of using Trending Topics in brand Tweets,
we'll need to build out a dataset that allows us to see when brands are
using these micro-trends. Here's how I did that:

1. Starting with our collection of Tweets from 100+ brands over the
   past few years, I removed all retweets and replies from the data set.
   We are only interested in Tweets that are created by the brand and
   intended for a wide audience. Because the query that I'll describe
   below is fairly complicated, I limited the data set to the past year's
   worth of data.

2. I then cross-referenced the content of each Tweet with a list of
   Trending Topics from Twitter. I limited the matches to the same
   day (so for every Trending Topic that occurred on Twitter in the
   past year in the United States, I checked each brand Tweet to see
   if the trend was included in any brand content). So, in the end,
   I ended up with a list of brand Tweets from the past year that
   included a Twitter Trending Topic in the United States and a list
   of brand Tweets that did not include one.

3. I took one more important step before checking the results. We've
   already seen a few anecdotal examples of a few brands doing real-
   time marketing during large events with huge success, and I didn't
   want those results skewing this data set. What I was interested

in seeing with this analysis was how including *every day* trends impacts performance, and not just any Twitter Trending Topic. So, as one last step, I removed all data from days in which large tent-pole events occurred, the same events that we will analyze in the next chapter. This gets us to more of an everyday data view to gauge performance and will make sure those big outliers aren't messing with our data. Sound good? Good.

So for one year's worth of Tweets (April 1, 2013—April 1, 2014), with all content removed from days in which one of our large events took place, I ended up with about 77,000 Tweets from brands that contained original content. The data shows that brands are using Trending Topics on Twitter, but not as a routine practice. In fact, for the year's worth of data I looked at, only 6 percent (about 4,900 Tweets) of the content during that time included a term that trended across the United States.

A few of the brands using everyday Trending Topics with the highest frequency include:

- Visa: 29 percent of original content
- Facebook: 29 percent of original content
- Heineken: 20 percent of original content
- Duracell: 19 percent of original content
- Burberry: 14 percent of original content
- Budweiser: 13 percent of original content.

While only 6 percent of the total content included a Trending Topic, a vast majority of the brands in our study had included at least one trending topics in their Twitter content. Out of the total of 106 brands, 103 had at least one Tweet using a hashtag or phrase that trended on the same day as they created their content. Here's a quick look at how brands use Trending Topics:

Hashtags versus Phrases

When we compare brands using trending hashtags versus trending words and phrases, we see that brands tend to gravitate slightly more toward hashtags. While Twitter's Trending Topics for the United States broke down pretty evenly at 48 percent hashtags and 52 percent words/phrases during the time of this study, 55 percent of the trends that brands included in their Twitter content used a hashtag, while 45 percent used a word or phrase that was trending at the time. So this is not that big of a difference. Why, then, are we talking about it? You'll find out in a minute.

Content Patterns

Many brands are jumping on the same Trending Topics with similar patterns. Some of the top trends used by brands during this year fall into some interesting groups:

- **locations**: "America," "London," "New York," and other geographic names were used in high frequency by brands when trending
- **breaking news**: discussions and mentions of topical events all saw a good amount of content created by brands
- **social media micro-trends**: "#tbt" and "#throwbackthursday" were both used in high frequency, a trend in which users post information that recalls retro moments from years ago

TRENDING TOPIC PERFORMANCE

So while most brands have included Trending Topics in their Tweets during the time frame of this study, not all include this content as a regular practice. So should brands be doing this more?

Our data set indicates that the practice is showing an very positive impact for brands (Figure 2.17). When brands include a Trending Topic in their Tweet, when not controlling for any other variables, they see a big boost in sharing and engagement. Retweets per follower for Tweets with Trending Topics see a 99 percent bump and favorites per follower see an 81 percent bump when compared to content that does not mention a trend.

A few of the top brands that see performance bumps using this practice include Amazon's Twitter content, which sees a 139 percent higher retweet per follower and a 122 percent higher favorite per

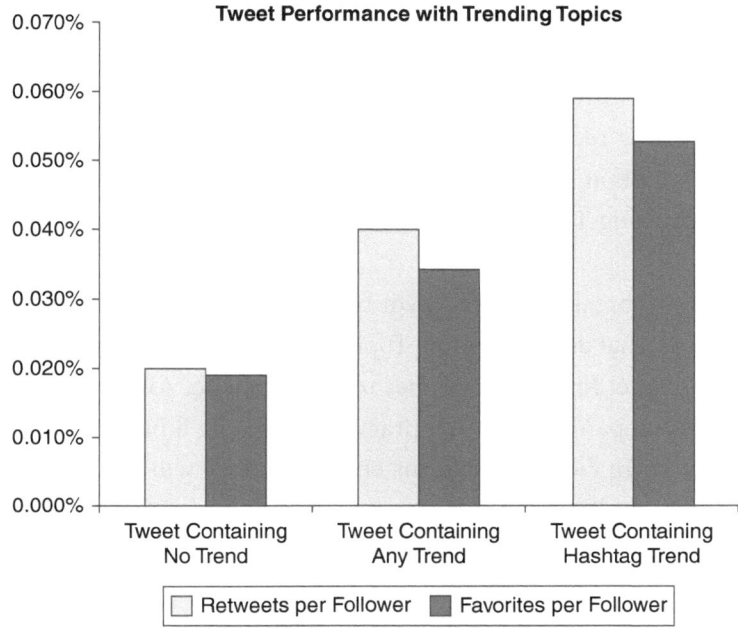

Figure 2.17 Tweet performance with brands using Trending Topics with and without hashtags

follower versus their other Tweets. Burberry is seeing a 92 percent bump to retweets and a 105 percent bump in favorites when including a Trending Topic in their content. It seems that jumping on relevant topics provides a big boost for brands, and that the audience is along for the ride.

And remember when we looked at companies using Trending Topics and how they only slightly favor hashtags? Well, brands that look at performance numbers might want to rethink that strategy. Figure 2.17 also shows that Tweets with hashtag Trending Topics see close to a 50 percent bump in both retweets per follower and favorites per follower. This pattern follows on the individual level as well—with both the brands mentioned above seeing great results from their hashtag trend usage. Budweiser, in fact, is enjoying a 100 percent+ bump in performance for both metrics when comparing hashtag trends versus nonhashtag trends.

Overall, the data leads us to believe this tactic is working, but let's not just settle for top-level averages. We want to look at the distribution of performance across brands to make sure a few rock stars that are doing really well aren't obscuring our view of reality. To do that, let's look at every individual brand and the performance each sees when using Trending Topics (specifically hashtag trends) in their Tweets.

When we break the data down by performance per brand (Figure 2.18), we see that using Trending Topics is providing an overwhelmingly positive impact for the companies using the tactic. Almost 70 percent of the 93 companies using the practice are seeing a bump in retweets per follower. In fact, two patterns emerge that we will continue seeing throughout multiple examples as we examine real-time marketing in this book:

1. Real-time marketing is showing positive performance in a wide majority of the cases that we examine.
2. The gains the majority of brands see from real-time marketing are far greater than the losses a few brands are seeing.

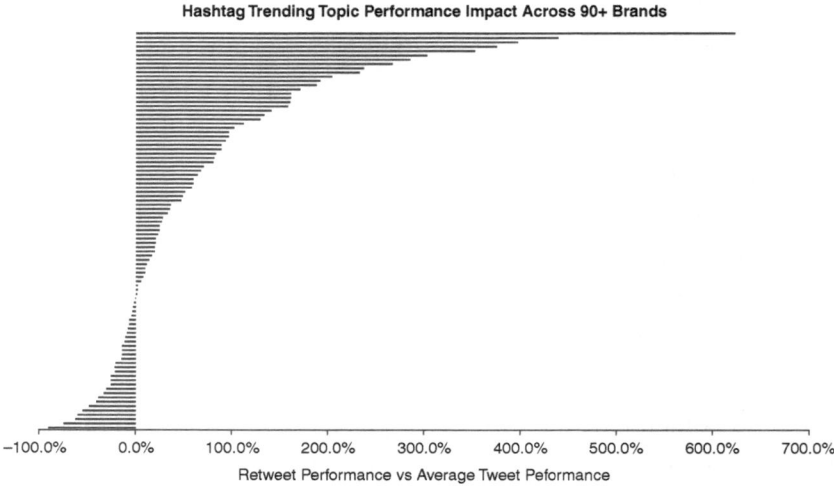

Figure 2.18 Retweets per follower performance when using Trending Topics in Tweets, per brand

I call this shape the *RTM Wave* (because it looks a bit like a wave about to crest), and it's something that we'll see repeatedly in the next few chapters. Across many different forms of RTM, there is a big upside and a small downside, and most brands are finding themselves on the positive side of the equation.

LEARN, PLAN, AND EXPERIMENT

So, we've had some fun with our data, and taken a good look at not only how brands are using Twitter today but also what's working for brands. You now know more than when you started reading this chapter about tactics that work for brands on Twitter, and what might work for your brand as well. Hashtags seem like a pretty good idea. Trending Topics seem even better. Question marks? Not so much.

But remember, while you should use these findings as an indicator of what might bring success, it's not a guarantee that it will work for your brand. All brands are different. What works for Nike might not work for Kia. What works for a financial brand like Visa might not resonate with the CPG audience that Tide speaks to each and every day on social media. Use these examples as ideas that your social media team can pepper into your current strategy, measure the results, and then decide whether these tactics should be a permanent fixture in your social plan.

ON TO THE REAL-TIME

We've established a good baseline for how brands use Twitter, and how the audience responds to different tactics across a wide sample of brands. These are high-level findings across all of our brands, but we need to go another level deeper to make these insights actionable.

In the next few chapters we'll do exactly that—we'll dive in each of our RTM quadrants (Planned, Watchlist, Opportunistic, and Every Day) to see what works and what doesn't. We'll learn how the audience reacts to Trending Topics in different scenarios and translate what we learn into tactics that marketers can use to boost their own performance. Who's excited?

This page intentionally left blank

Chapter 3

RTM PERFORMANCE FOR BIG, KNOWN EVENTS

AS MARKETERS WONDER WHETHER THEY SHOULD invest in real-time marketing, there are plenty of anecdotes to base their decisions on—from Oreo to Arby's to Samsung's Ellen selfie—but not much data to help them out. What about the success of brands that didn't make the headlines from their social efforts during a big, tent-pole event? How are the social teams that didn't "win" the event, even after spending long hours preparing for and executing social strategies, feeling about their success with RTM? Is the audience paying attention? What can brands and media companies do to improve their RTM results? With all the press that RTM has received to date, I've seen a lot of opinions, theories, and arguments from both sides, but there's not a lot of data.

In the last chapter, we took a look at how brands are using Twitter with different methods of communication, and looked at some success factors that are proving to be more effective for some brands. We built out a baseline for what success looks like on Twitter for most brands, both with raw numbers and our much preferred "actions per follower" KPIs. We not only looked at how to measure success but also dove into what works for brands in aggregate to promote more sharing and engagement from the audience. And hopefully we brought some data-driven thinking to tactics that have, in the past, been driven by gut instinct.

Figure 3.1   The Real-Time Marketing Matrix

We saw that brands are enjoying an overall lift in social performance by leveraging trends, but now let's dive deeper into big tent-pole events (like the Oscars, the Super Bowl, the Grammys, etc.) that bring so much attention along with them.

In this chapter, we'll look into the two event-based quadrants of the RTM Matrix that we can see on the left-hand side of Figure 3.1 (Planned RTM and Opportunistic RTM) and use Twitter data to analyze the performance of each. This is the first step in our journey to figure out if real-time marketing makes sense for brands to invest in—is it worth all the effort of building out a team, the planning, executing, and analyzing? Does RTM, when we look across a wide spectrum of brands in different verticals and with different brand voices, work with any consistency across big events? Does it work for preplanned content better than seat-of-the-pants responses?

We're finally going to bring some data to real-time marketing for big events. Buckle up.

THE THEORY OF TENT-POLE EVENTS AND SOCIAL

Let's start with a theory. And that theory is that real-time marketing during large events makes sense for one main reason: *attention*. A few times a year, there are seismic ripples of attention in the marketing universe. These are big pop culture events that each bring such enormous reach that marketers line up for the chance to get their message across to the audience. In 2014, Nielsen numbers estimated that 111 million viewers watched the Super Bowl, or approximately 35 percent of the entire population of the United States.

When you step back and think about it, this is a really big deal. When's the last time you could get your group of five coworkers together for a drink after work without someone having to skip out for yoga or day-care pickup or whatever else they do? I can't remember the last time I could get both of my kids to listen to a recap about my day at work for more than ten seconds, but big events like these capture the thoughts of more than one-third of the United States over a few hours time. That's a huge number of households tuned in to the same second-by-second action, talking about that crazy thing that just happened, asking the same questions, or laughing at the same jokes in unison. It's been a huge opportunity for marketers, and even more so now that social media has given brands the ability to communicate in real-time. Social has given marketers a new avenue and new opportunity to engage the audience, and a real-time platform truly adds something special to the equation.

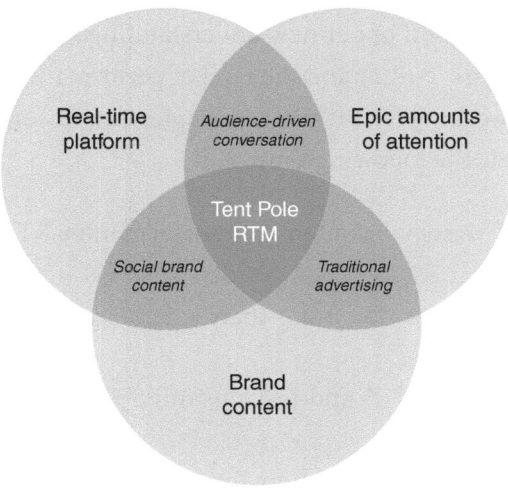

Figure 3.2   The theory of tent-pole RTM, visualized

Historically, advertising and sponsorships have been the obvious way for marketers to take advantage of these huge tent-pole events and the attention they bring. As viewership has risen over the years, the price for the privilege of getting that attention has gone through the roof. A 30-second spot during the 2014 Super Bowl reportedly went for north of $4 million dollars. But, like we discussed earlier, social is a different animal. Social media's conversation-based medium gives it certain advantages that make it a great channel during these large events (and as we'll see later, smaller micro-events as well).

THE OPPORTUNITY

If the theory of real-time marketing is correct, there is a huge opportunity for marketers to increase the performance of their social content by increasing their relevance to the audience. By jumping in on the attention that is already directed at a certain topic, brands can capture some of that value by simply joining the conversation. If the theory is correct, smart marketers should be able to blend art and science to make the most of the opportunity.

Let's look at real-time marketing content from big events over the past few years and see how it stacks up to other content. We'll cut the data in a few different ways to try and understand what works and what doesn't. We'll build off of our new understanding from the last chapter on how brands use Twitter and the level of performance they receive to see if RTM is working for them. This chapter details some RTM analysis to investigate the following aspects:

- Does RTM social content outperform non-RTM social content?
- Does RTM work for more than a few brands at big, tent-pole events?
- How effective is Brand-to-Consumer RTM versus Brand-to-Brand RTM?
- How does truly in-the-moment content (Opportunistic RTM) during big events stack up against Planned RTM content?

Or said another way: does bringing your social team in on Sunday to live-tweet the Grammys actually do anything for your brand's social performance? Good question. Let's find out.

MEASUREMENT

We'll measure RTM performance using metrics that should be starting to look familiar. All brands in our data set created Twitter content that allows us to measure engagement (via favorites) and social sharing (via retweets). In a similar fashion to the analysis we've been doing in this book, we will also normalize the success metrics to make this a fair fight between brands—we certainly don't want brands with unusually large or small follower sets skewing the data in any direction. Basically, we'll be using the same methodology as we did for our brands in the Twitter baseline study. We'll go one step further here—in this chapter we'll also look at follower growth as a measure of performance. Follower growth is a valuable goal for companies—every additional follower for a brand on Twitter helps a brand increase reach with every future Tweet. This equates to real value for companies, so we'll add it to our list.

THE DATA

From the data side, we'll start with our database of brand Tweets, but we'll need to identify real-time marketing Tweets versus other brand content. Some of this will have to be done by hand—this takes some legwork, but isn't all that difficult. We're not exactly splitting the atom here, and I'll walk you through the simple way I went about doing this.

First, I identified the "major events" we are interested in for this study. I selected major tent-pole events that receive a huge amount of media attention and television ratings, and events that had a good amount brands creating RTM content during the event. The event list ended up as follows: the Super Bowl, the Oscars, the Golden Globes, and the Grammys. Our data set includes content for these events across both 2013 and 2014.

Next, I identified the RTM Tweets that our 100+ brands created during these tent-pole events. If you'll remember from chapter 1, there are two main buckets of RTM for big events: Planned and Opportunistic. We grab the data for those two categories of content in very different ways.

PLANNED RTM

As a large event approaches, marketers know a few things about what's going to happen. Generally they know the major story lines going into the event (a big game where two players from opposing teams dislike each other, a famous actor has been snubbed for an Oscar consistently over the past few years, etc.); they know when the event will start; they know certain micro-events might happen during the event (one of five different singers will win Best New Artist this year); and many other "known" topics. Social media teams can, and do, build content around many of these known themes to post during the event as it happens, in addition to any other RTM that's being created on the fly. This is the content we're calling Planned RTM.

To identify this RTM content, I relied on a combination of date stamps and hashtags for each tent-pole event. For example, for the 2014 Super Bowl, I included every brand Tweet from our 100+ brands that tweeted on the day of the Super Bowl with a related hashtag or trending topic ("#SB28," "#SuperBowl," "Super Bowl," etc.) I excluded the Opportunistic RTM content in this data set to avoid cross-contamination of our data, which will allow us to compare the two tactics. After pulling all the data across big events, I identified around 700 Tweets from our brands that qualify as Planned RTM brand content.

OPPORTUNISTIC RTM

During a big event, there are smaller events that happen and couldn't be predicted. During the opening coin flip for the 2014 Super Bowl, for example, Joe Namath came out onto the field wearing a huge, crazy-looking fur coat. No one saw that coming (except, I'm guessing, Mr. Namath), and that's an example of a micro-event happening within the larger event. Any content based off of these types of micro-trends is what we're calling Opportunistic RTM.

Identifying this type of content is, unfortunately, a manual process. Here are the steps I took to identify and classify Opportunistic RTM Tweets:

1. Starting with our 300,000+ plus brand Tweets, I removed all retweets and replies. These are interesting for certain forms of social media analysis, but not relevant for real-time marketing efforts that are generally original content created by a brand and intended for the entire audience to see. Now we're looking at 117,000+ tweets from 106 brands.

2. I identified the Tweets that were posted by our brands on the days of our target events.

3. I manually reviewed each brand Tweet containing original content from the day of each event. If a Tweet was about a real-time micro-event ("Touchdown!"=yes) and not just a generic brand message ("Enjoying the Oscars? Try our cereal."=no), it was marked as RTM. Yes, this was tedious work, but it's what I'm here for.

4. I merged this data back into the database. We now have all RTM content for big events from 2013 and 2014 labeled as such, and we can segment and query the data as needed.

Pretty straightforward. After applying this criteria and scoring the Tweets, I see that 56 of our 108 brands, or 52 percent, have tweeted at least one Opportunistic real-time marketing message during a large event over the past few years, creating a total of over 850 Opportunistic RTM Tweets from our brands.

So between our Planned RTM and Opportunistic RTM data sets, we have around 1,500 brand Tweets with which to measure the performance of RTM. Not a huge data set, but real-time marketing is a relatively new practice, so that's to be expected. Let's break this down a few different ways to see what this data can tell us.

BIG EVENTS: PLANNED RTM PERFORMANCE

First, we'll look at how our Planned RTM performed over the eight tent-pole events our data set covers. Is the audience responding to

	Brand Average	Planned RTM	
Retweets per Follower	0.017%	0.085%	**+400%**
Favorites per Follower	0.014%	0.073%	**+421%**

Figure 3.3 The performance of Planned RTM vs. average Tweet performance for brands

prebuilt content around big events? Turns out that on average they are.

Figure 3.3 shows that Planned RTM content, like brands using the "#SuperBowl" hashtag during the game, shows an average 399 percent bump in retweets per follower and a 413 percent bump in favorites per follower versus non-RTM social content from brands. But when we look at the distribution of performance across our brands, we find out that Planned RTM doesn't work in every case. Of the 40 brands that created Planned RTM content for the tent-pole events in this study, 23 (or 58%) of them saw positive performance bumps. Some of the brands seeing the largest Known RTM performance bumps were Duracell, Disney, and Budweiser. The gains are far outweighing the losses for brands, but the split is just slightly in favor of brands seeing increases in performance.

So just creating content with a mention of a big event doesn't necessarily guarantee success with social performance, but the majority of brands are seeing an overall increase to average retweet and favorite numbers. But just wait until we look at the Opportunistic RTM performance numbers.

BIG EVENTS: OPPORTUNISTIC RTM PERFORMANCE

When it comes to brands truly creating, building and posting on-the-fly Tweets around micro-events within tent-pole events, the data shows that the performance impact is positive on a very consistent basis.

Opportunistic RTM content shows even more impressive results, with more than an average 1,200 percent lift for retweets per follower and a 1,100 percent lift for favorites per follower when compared with

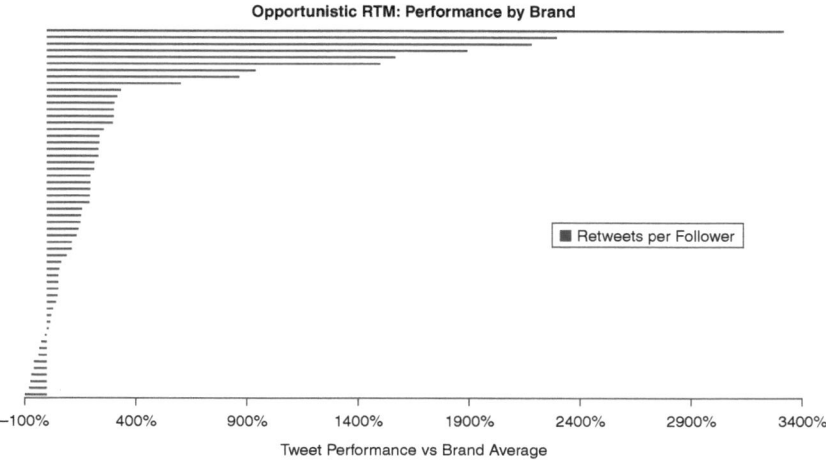

Figure 3.4 Opportunistic RTM performance, by individual brand vs. average Tweet

its normal brand social equivalent. When we look at the distribution of performance brand by brand across 56 brands doing Opportunistic RTM in Figure 3.4, the RTM wave shape returns.

The data tells us that the success of Opportunistic real-time marketing isn't just concentrated in the shining stars that you read about the next day. Eighty-two percent, or 46 of the 56 brands engaging in RTM with unknown content, see a higher average retweet per follower and favorites per follower versus their normal social content. This even includes some of the brands in the study that only created one piece of RTM content during a large event in our sample time frame (including Allianz, Discovery, and Intel.) The data shows that RTM can work across a diverse set of brands, not just a few within certain industries or brands with a particular kind of voice.

Remember what we've heard—real-time marketing is just a flash in the pan. It can't be repeated. It won't work for every brand. It's not worth the effort. Your brand will just look silly trying to be relevant in a sea of other brands, all just vying for the attention of a an audience that doesn't care. The data we're seeing across many brands and 1,500 RTM Tweets (summarized in Figure 3.5) now tells us, maybe not.

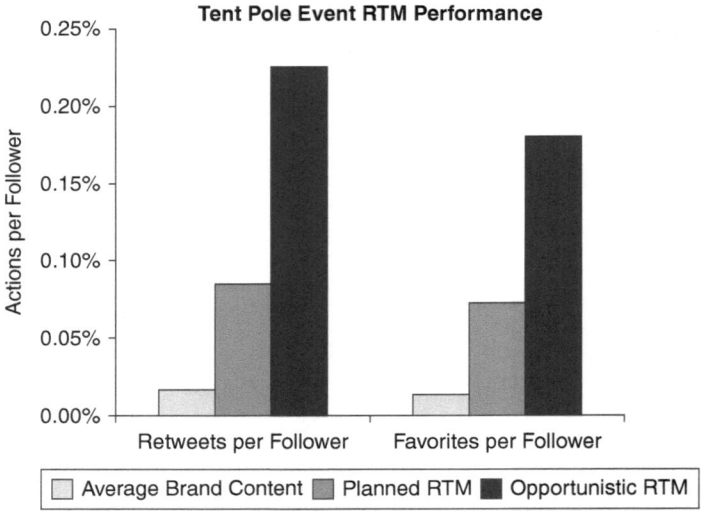

Figure 3.5 Engagement performance of normal brand social content compared to tent-pole, real-time marketing social content, measured by ratio of actions per follower

So now that we've confirmed that real-time marketing is performing pretty consistently across the majority of brands we're looking at, let's analyze another myth that gets discussed frequently by RTM critics—that only one brand can "win" each event.

TENT-POLE RTM PERFORMANCE: ONE WINNER PER EVENT?

For the past few years after each large, tent-pole event, we've consistently heard the same few things the next morning from the press—the media's take on which brand "won" social the night before. Real-time marketing has become an undercard to the main event, and everyone rushes to declare a single victor who had the best Tweets, posts, and real-time responses as the event played out. While it's fun to keep up with the marketing subculture of winners and losers, it also unfortunately underscores the feeling that each event can only have one brand that benefits from real-time marketing. So, is this really the case?

Well, let's begin with the definition of a "social winner." For the sake of this book, I'll frame this concept as any brand that receives a huge amount of social response for one or more Tweets that they send out during the event, as compared to their normal Tweet performance. We'll actually set the bar pretty high here and say that we'll declare a superstar Tweet as any RTM content (Planned or Opportunistic) with more than 1,000 retweets or favorites. To give you an idea of how rare this feat is, after looking through our brand Tweet data set, only 1,410 Tweets out of our 117,000 in the study achieved this level of response. The 1,000 interaction count level represents the top 1 percent of all original brand Tweets for engagement and sharing—those sounds like winners to me.

Now let's look at each event in our timeline and see how many superstar Tweets appeared during each event from RTM. Is the Oreo moment a one-time thing, or is there room for more than one brand to hit a grand slam during big worldwide events?

As you can see in Figure 3.6, real-time marketing during large events isn't just limited to one champion per match. The majority of events are showing multiple brands with stellar success in getting their RTM content shared. As it turns out, real-time marketing isn't a winner-take-all effort. It can, and usually does, create multiple "one-in-a-million" moments for brands during the same event.

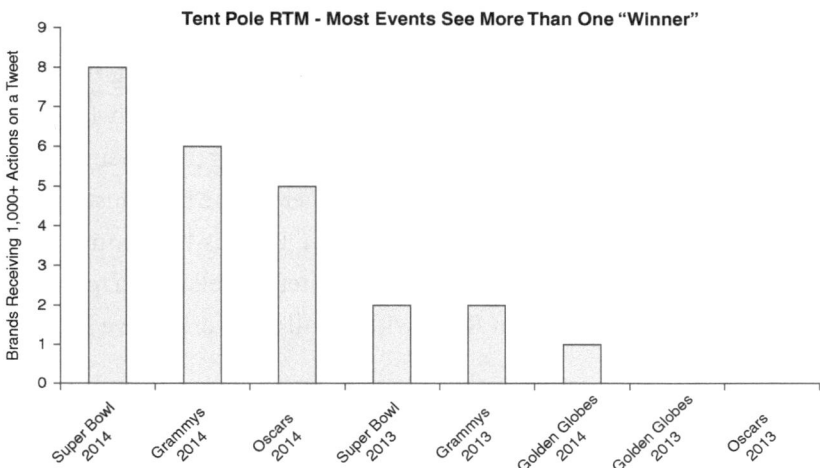

Figure 3.6 Big social winners per tent-pole event

GREAT, SO I SHOULD JUST POST SOCIAL
CONTENT DURING BIG EVENTS?

Don't worry. I can already hear the gears turning in your head:

> *Tweets during large events get a better response than other social media that brands create during the year…okay. You know, that's not really that surprising. I bet that the audience is responding to social media in higher numbers during the Super Bowl because there are just more people paying attention to Twitter during the Super Bowl.*
>
> *None of this increased performance is actually about RTM. It's just about putting a message, any kind of message, out there during a large tent-pole event, and I'll get the same return. It's the social media equivalent of shooting fish in a barrel, and I can schedule this social content three weeks before the event and give my social media team the day off.*

These are all good points, you. Let's check the data to see if this is indeed the case.

So how do we look at the data to show that real-time marketing is the big winner here, and not just any social posted during a big event? We'll take a look at all social content posted by our 100 brands during large events, and check the performance of RTM content (Planned and Opportunistic) versus any other social content during the events. That is to say, if you tweet a generic, off-topic brand message during the Super Bowl—something that is precanned and doesn't even acknowledge the tent-pole event—will it get the same lift as something that's being generated from micro-events from within the larger event? Does just the fact that the Oscars, the Grammys, or the Super Bowl is happening at the same time lift the performance of brand content? Well, if you're looking to get the performance from RTM without all the work…I've got good news and bad news.

The Good News: The good news for you, lazy marketer, is that scheduled, non-real-time social posts during large events do in fact perform better than other branded social content. The numbers are actually pretty good. Social content that is not about a big event, and just happens to be posted during the event, receives 2× the retweets and favorites on average versus normal levels. That's pretty great performance and a great stat to know. But there's bad news as well.

The Bad News: The bad news is that even if you get a performance bump from creating and posting scheduled social posts during large events, you're still missing out. In fact, you're missing out on a ton of performance gains that could be found by using real-time marketing during these events.

Across the eight events I analyzed, all but one (the 2013 Grammys) showed brands seeing a higher average retweet rate for real-time marketing content versus other branded content posted during the event (Figure 3.7). And RTM didn't just edge out the other brand content—it crushed it. On average, real-time marketing content received 630 percent more retweets per follower versus other branded content during the same event, and favorites per follower was closely behind with 400 percent higher engagement.

So what happened during the Grammys in 2013? Well, first of all, we had a very small sample—only 14 total Tweets in our sample, which

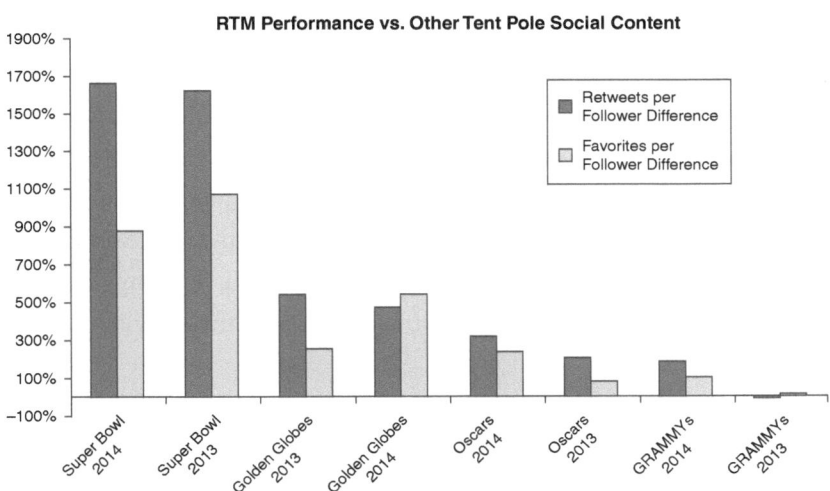

Figure 3.7 RTM Performance for big events vs. other brand social content posted during the event

were split down the middle, resulting in just seven RTM Tweets and seven non-RTM Tweets. But it was more about the content—not as many brands jumped on in-the-moment events, our Opportunistic quadrant that performs so well, during the awards show.

If you're looking to repeat the success that many brands have seen with real-time marketing, simply posting premade social content during big events might give you a bump, but it won't take full advantage of the true RTM opportunity. It's not enough to Tweet out a link to your latest commercial or ask the audience a few generic questions during the Oscars—if you're looking to capture the attention of your followers, you need to be on point and creating content on the fly.

TENT-POLE RTM PERFORMANCE: FOLLOWER GROWTH

Building a strong follower base is a goal for many brands, so let's take a look at how real-time marketing during tent-pole events impacts attracting new followers for brands. After we pull the data for brands creating RTM content (either Planned or Opportunistic), the outliers show phenomenal results in this category. Oreo's Tweet during the 2013 Super Bowl increased their follower count by 21 percent over just a few days. Or said another way, because of their RTM efforts, Oreo's Super Bowl Tweet was able to grow their Twitter audience by the same number of followers as their *previous six months of work*. DiGiorno was able to grow their Twitter audience by 14 percent (or about 8,000 followers) over a few days by utilizing real-time marketing tactics during the 2014 Super Bowl. These two examples are impressive, and similar to the "shining star" type of analysis we see in the media about all the social media winners after each big event.

But these are outliers—what we want to know is what is the overall performance of RTM follower growth. Do all brands see a lift in Twitter followers after a big event, just due to more people being on Twitter? Does RTM success with follower growth stop with the superstars?

If we look at a sample of ten brands doing real-time marketing and not doing real-time marketing during a few large events, the overall

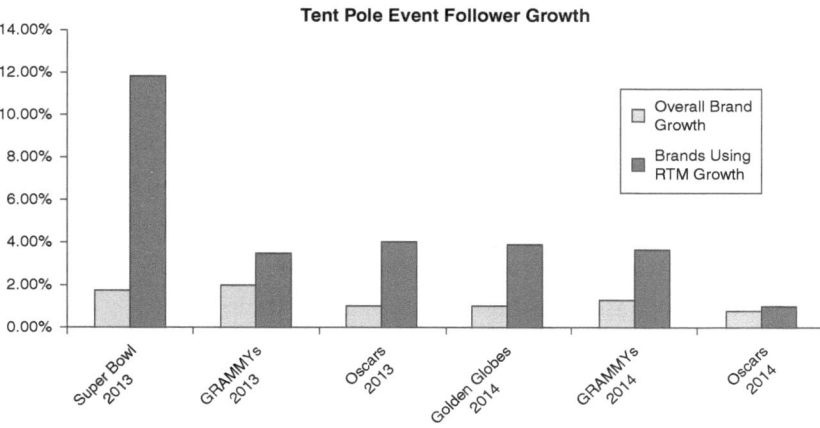

Figure 3.8 RTM Follower growth vs. other brand Follower growth during tent-pole events

pattern still favors RTM. Figure 3.8 shows a view covering multiple events:

As you can see, brands using RTM (either Planned or Opportunistic) during these large events did far better in follower growth over every single event in the past two years. The average brand doing RTM during one of these events earned 359 percent more followers on average than brands not doing RTM during those events. And while sharing and engagement are great short-term spikes of social success, follower growth can benefit a brand or media company for years to come, opening up a wider channel of communication for all its future Tweets.

So overall engagement and sharing metrics are higher, and follower numbers are impressive as well. We're making a pretty good case for brands to engage in tent-pole real-time marketing. But let's slice this data a few more ways to try and poke a few holes in it.

BRANDS TALKING TO BRANDS—DOES IT WORK?

So as we discussed in chapter 1, real-time marketing has evolved into not only messages that contain original content about a trend but also include content reaching out to other brands. During large events, brands will tweet at other brands—usually ones that are also involved in real-time marketing during the same time period—to try to elicit some sort of social reaction. When it works, multiple brands chiming in on the same joke can be amusing and sharable content for the audience. When it falls flat, it can be a little embarrassing—the social media equivalent of a high five that is never returned. This cross-pollination of content normally manifests itself in a few ways:

- mentioning or calling out another brand as part of the content, such as John Deere's mentioning Pepsi for whatever reason
- making fun of another brand's real-time activities, but usually in a lighthearted manner
- recognizing other brands during the tent-pole event for good real-time marketing content

How can we use a data-driven approach to understand and even predict which brands might reach out and connect with others during a large tent-pole event? We'll take a quick look with a set of concepts known as social network analysis (SNA). SNA looks at the relationships between individuals to see if they are connected to each other (in the case of Twitter, we'll check to see which brands are following each other). Once we collect data to map out all these different relationships

Figure 3.9   Kia engaging in Brand-to-Brand Real-Time Marketing by calling out JCPenney, which was tweeting incoherent messages as part of their "Tweeting With Mittens" micro-campaign during the 2014 Super Bowl

between the brands, we can analyze connection patterns to gain insights from the number of links between brands, identify groups and subgroups, and measure influence.

I grabbed data about our 100+ brands to find out which brands each brand is following and ended up with what looks like a spider's web of connections. What this data set gives us is an understanding of brands that are monitoring each other's social media activity, what patterns those connections make at a high level, and what we can infer about relationships from the connections. Figure 3.10 shows a quick look at how our 100+ brands are connected on Twitter.

To go beyond just viewing the overall map of connections, we can run a few SNA measurements to understand which brands would be most likely to talk with each other during a big event.

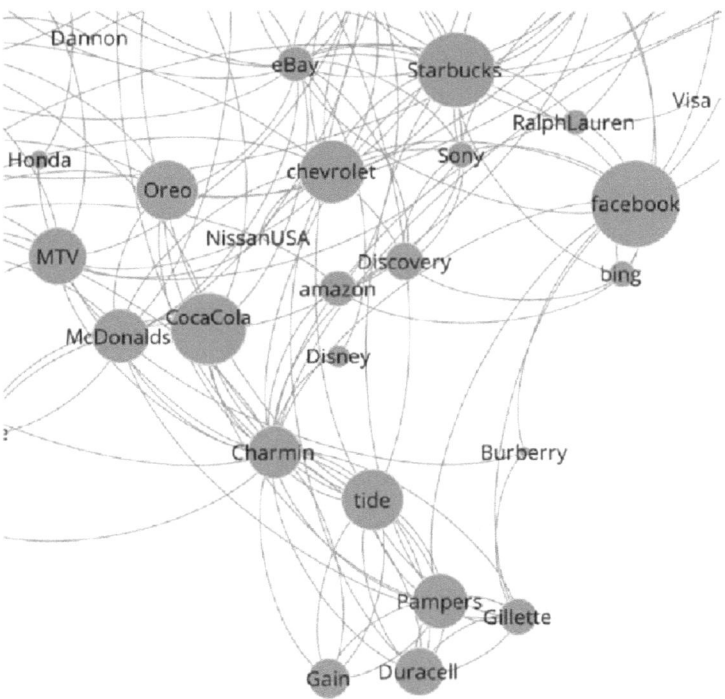

Figure 3.10 A social network analysis (SNA) mapping of brands following other brands on Twitter

MOST FOLLOWED BRANDS (BY OTHER BRANDS)

Brands often follow other brands on Twitter to keep track of their posting behavior and themes. We can see the most popular brands through a measure called "in-degree centrality," or more simply put, the brands with the most other brands following them on Twitter.

The top brands being followed by other brands on Twitter are:

- Facebook: followed by 13 brands
- Starbucks: followed by 13 brands
- MTV: followed by 11 brands
- Oreo: followed by 9 brands
- Coca-Cola: followed by 9 brands

Well, you can go ahead and say it—that's kind of weird. From the group of brands in this study, Facebook is one of the most-followed brands...on Twitter. Bet you didn't see that coming. The other names on the top-five list are extremely well-known brands who have historically been very active on social media. So these are the cool kids—the brands that others are following the most.

BRANDS FOLLOWING OTHER BRANDS

What about a look at the other direction—a look to find the most social brands with other brands? Or, said another way, which brands follow the most other brands on our list?

The top brands following other brands on Twitter are

- Charmin: following 20 other brands
- eBay: following 16 other brands
- HP: following 15 other brands
- VW: following 13 other brands
- Butterfinger: following 13 other brands

These are the brands most interested in the social activity of other brands, which is a better indicator of brands that will potentially reach out to other brands with RTM. In fact, four of these top five have indeed engaged in Brand-to-Brand RTM over the past few years.

So if you're a brand that is looking to include this tactic in your future efforts, you can use a similar strategy to identify brands that are most likely to respond back to your efforts. It's easy to track down brands that traditionally engage in Brand-to-Brand RTM, but you can take it one step further to make sure your content has a better chance of sparking a conversation. You should be targeting not only brands that are connected to your own brand on Twitter but also companies that are more connected with other brands that might make a good conversation partner.

So now that we know which brands are the most active in following other brands, let's get to the important question: should brands being doing this at all?

BRAND-TO-BRAND RTM: ARE AUDIENCES ALONG FOR THE RIDE?

These real-time marketing brand-to-brand sideshows have created a very strange environment for anyone paying attention during large events. It's unknown how many people in the audience are actually in on the joke, and whether they truly understand that brands are trying to position themselves as part of the show. It turns out that almost 10 percent of all the RTM content in this study is made up of brand-to-brand communication (which is meant to be consumed by the masses), which represents a material amount of chatter. Is this just some inside-baseball-type content, for which it's only purpose is to amuse the social media teams working on Super Bowl Sunday? Or are audiences on board, engaging and sharing the content that is created through these brand-level conversations?

The data tells us that all that brand chatter, at least with our limited data set, isn't paying off. RTM Tweets that included brand-to-brand communication performed worse than other Opportunistic RTM content, showing 59 percent fewer retweets per follower and 56 percent fewer favorites per follower. While brands might consider their inter-brand banter amusing within our little industry, on average the audience is tuning out.

CELEBRITY MESSAGES AND CALLOUTS

Another tactic that brands use while engaging in real-time marketing during tent-pole events is attempting to use celebrity mentions to increase their content effectiveness. Brands frequently mention famous personalities in different contexts. Brands commonly mention the celebrity's social media handle when he or she wins an award or performs well during a big event. Alternatively, some brands mention a A-listers with the off-chance that he or she might respond during the event. Alas, a response rarely materializes, but still celebrity mentions make up almost 25 percent of the tent-pole RTM content in this study.

So, yes, it's happening. But is this tactic working to achieve good performance in sharing and engagement? Again, not so much.

RTM content in which brands mention celebrity Twitter handles or names performs worse than the average real-time marketing content. The content showed performance lagging far behind other Opportunistic RTM, with 47 percent fewer retweets per follower and 35 percent fewer favorites per follower. So while mentioning celebrities might be fun for the social media teams running these efforts, the fans and followers prefer it when brands leave out the A-listers altogether.

HASHTAGS IN TENT-POLE RTM CONTENT

Hashtags were used in 88 percent of our tent-pole RTM Tweets, making it a widely-used tool for brands during events. Many brands use event-driven hashtags to identify themselves as being in on the conversation (such as "#Oscars," "#SuperBowl," and "#GoldenGlobes"), but others use personalized hashtags that they'd like to see their audience echo. A few examples:

- Digiorno used the #DiGiorNOYOUDIDNT hashtag with its 2014 Super Bowl Tweets to add a recurring punch line to their all-caps one-liners.
- KFC hosted their own sideshow during the 2014 Oscars with a #BucketAwards hashtag that was designed to go viral.

- Microsoft's Bing search engine tweeted with the #BingOscars hashtag during the 2014 show.

So, do hashtags help move the performance needle? As we look through our data set, the findings point to yes. RTM Tweets with hashtags received, on average, 42 percent more retweets per follower and 60 percent more favorites per follower versus non-hashtagged real-time content across both Planned and Opportunistic RTM. Hashtag away, my friends.

OPPORTUNISTIC RTM: THE 2014 WORLD CUP

In the summer of 2014, the world's attention turned to football (or soccer, as we call it in the United States) as teams and fans from across the globe traveled to Brazil for the World Cup. Television networks carrying the event reported record ratings as fans cheered on their favorite teams in their living rooms as well as on social media. When Germany finally won the tournament, Twitter revealed that conversation on the social network had reached a peak of more than 618,000 Tweets per minute, the highest levels ever seen during an event.

Brands also showed up for the World Cup, especially around a strange event that happened during the match between Uruguay and Italy. Uruguay's Luis Suarez, while guarding Italy's Giorgio Chiellini, appeared to bite him on the shoulder, sending Chiellini to the ground.

As disbelief around the event circled the globe, brands jumped on the opportunity (as seen in Figure 3.11) to chime in on a trending topic. I measured the performance of ten brands—ranging from Trident to Whataburger to Major League Baseball—that created Opportunistic RTM around "the bite felt 'round the world'" to see if their creative executions were not only clever but also effective. The results were downright ridiculous.

All ten of the brands saw a huge bump in retweets versus their normal levels, with the outliers (McDonald's of Uruguay and Snickers) both skewing the results highly positive, to result in an average bump of over 339,000 percent. You read that right.

Figure 3.11   The Snickers Tweet jumping on the 2014 World Cup bite incident

But outliers can skew our understanding of normalcy, so we'll look at the distribution of all ten brands' performance (seen in Figure 3.12) to demonstrate the power of RTM. The median increase in performance for these ten brands was over 4,300 percent—not too shabby. As you can see, all brands saw huge performance bumps. These brands served up some great, relevant content and the audience...apologies in advance...ate it up.

PLANNED RTM: HOLIDAYS

Since the dawn of advertising, brands have coordinated marketing activities around events that their audience could see coming

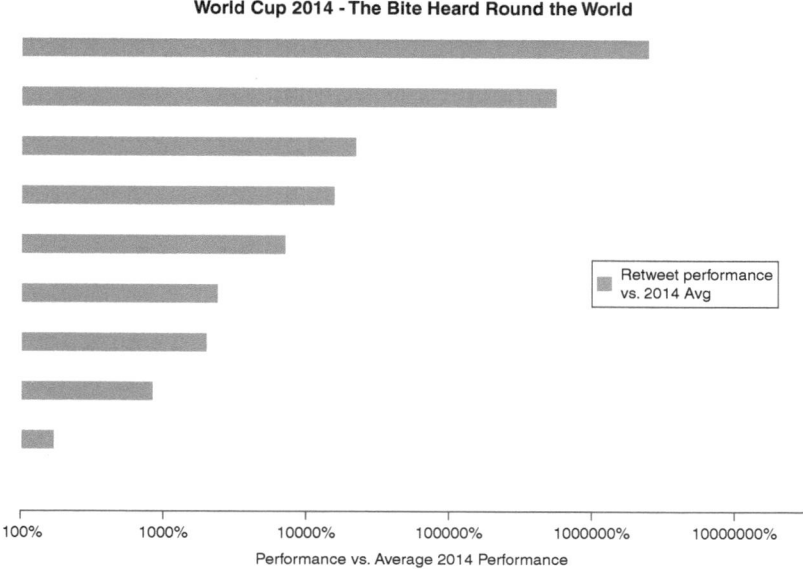

Figure 3.12 Retweet per follower performance across ten brands for RTM content about the World Cup bite

from miles away. These are events that not only happen every year but that usually include some type of commerce-based activity for brands to take advantage of. Christmas is the obvious big event for many companies, with retailers and brands competing for attention to make sure consumers consider their locations or products when buying gifts and anything else for the season. Other holidays, like Thanksgiving, the Fourth of July, and Mother's Day, also follow similar patterns, and huge campaigns revolve around getting in front of consumers with a pitch. Consumers understand these patterns and expect brands to compete for their attention with messaging, offers, and events (like Black Friday and Cyber Monday) each year.

Brands have jumped on these planned events via social media to stay relevant and take advantage of the attention these moments drive. In the era of overcommercialization and an ever-growing holiday season, it's natural for brands to be involved in conversations around major holidays. Consumers, it would seem, would be used to seeing brand messaging and offers in social channels around holidays—it's happening everywhere else, why not there as well? But as brands engage in a real-time manner around holiday topics, how does the audience react? Are followers coming along for the ride, or are these brands getting in the way of everyone's holiday celebrations? From the 100+ brands in our data set, I looked at Twitter Trending Topics holiday patterns in brand Tweets from April 2013 to April 2014. More specifically, I looked at brands that included hashtags or phrases that became Trending Topics in their content from the following set of holidays that are celebrated in the United States:

- **Valentine's Day** ("Valentine's Day," "Valentines," "#Valentines-Day," "ValentineCards")
- **St. Patrick's Day**("St. Patrick's Day," "Patricks," "#StPatricksDay," "HappyStPatricksDay")
- **Mother's Day** ("Mother's Day," "#MothersDay," "Happy Mother's Day")
- **The Fourth of July** ("4th of July," "#4thOfJuly," "July4th")
- **Halloween** ("Halloween," "#Halloween," "Happy Halloween," "#HappyHalloween")
- **Christmas** ("Christmas," "#Christmas," "Merry Christmas")
- **New Year's Eve/Day** ("New Year's Eve," "New Year," "New Years," "Happy New Year")

I then compared the performance of brands using the above Twitter Trending Topics in their Tweets versus their normal Tweet performance over the same time range. Does including a nice #MothersDay message in a Tweet boost sharing (retweets) and engagement (favorites) by the audience? You might be surprised.

THE HOLIDAY ROAD LOOKS BUMPY

If we look at the average performance of brand Tweets that include a holiday-themed Trending Topic, the numbers are encouraging at first glance. On average, brands see a 24 percent bump in retweets per follower and a 27 percent bump in favorites per follower when including holiday trends in their content. But, as we've talked about previously, high-level averages can skew what's actually going on inside the data set. If we take a closer look, we see a different story.

When comparing brand-by-brand performance (Figure 3.13), more brands see a *decrease* in Tweet performance when using a holiday Trending Topic in their Tweets. In fact, there wasn't one holiday in this study for which the brands seeing an increase in performance outnumbered the brands seeing a performance decrease. Real-time marketing, it seems, isn't as easy as that.

Why is this happening? Well, after looking through the social content, a lot of the Tweets that brands are posting for holidays are pretty uninspired. The content includes basic mentions of the holiday or themes, links to recipes that have been on their sites for years, and other ways to sneak a hashtag or topic into the audience's Twitter feed without putting much effort forward. It's the social media equivalent of just throwing a "Christmas!" banner across a regular print ad and expecting consumers

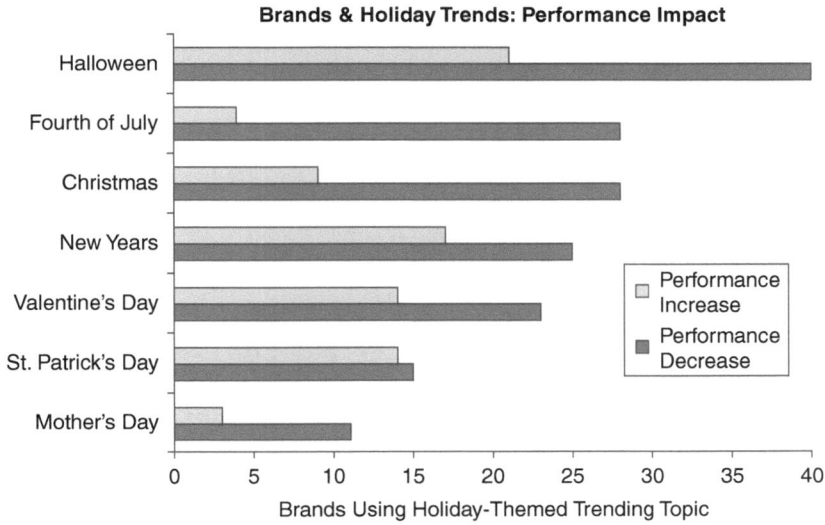

Figure 3.13   Holiday RTM performance by brands seeing a performance increase vs. decrease

to run to the store to check out their latest sales. When specialized creative is replaced with simple mentions of the holiday, the audience isn't impressed (and the numbers back that up.) When it comes to Planned RTM, holidays may very well be just too…planned.

That's not to say that *some* brands aren't seeing a performance bump. Here are a few brands with solid holiday performance and a few things we can learn from each:

Nintendo's Valentine's Day Tweet (Figure 3.14) saw a 732 percent increase in RTs and 1,154 percent increase in favorites versus its other social content during the year. It included prebuilt creative showing Mario and the Princess over the years, and, given Nintendo's primarily young audience, may have appealed to those who are most excited and tuned in during the V-day season.

Harley Davidson tweeted a great St. Patrick's Day photo of a hogriding, full-sized leprechaun, and their audience loved it. It saw a

Figure 3.14   Nintendo of America's Valentine's Day Tweet from 2014

Give us a RT if you'll be celebrating your baby's first Christmas this year. pic.twitter.com/GfjH3EdNPZ

↩ Reply ⇄ Retweet ★ Favorite ••• More

Figure 3.15   A holiday Tweet from @Pampers that received a big bump in shares

275 percent increase in retweets and 264 percent increase in favorites over their normal Twitter performance.

Pampers, by simply asking for retweets around baby's first Christmas (Figure 3.15), received a 451 percent bump in retweets per follower over their normal levels. Asking for the right gift during the holiday season seems to work.

Tide created a custom Vine with a "Paranormal Activity" theme for Halloween (that was actually kind of scary), and the result was a 465 percent bump in retweets and 318 percent increase in favorites versus their normal level of performance.

So brands can make holidays work, but simply including the Trending Topic for a holiday in your content probably isn't going to get you where you want to go. Taking advantage of the benefits of real-time doesn't just include being somewhat on topic and timing the communication for the right day. There's more that needs to be done in order for audiences to respond in a positive manner. Brands need both to understand the topic that is top of mind and create compelling content around the subject. Real-time marketing is a combination of art and science—and knowing the right time to engage is just one piece of the puzzle if you're looking to boost your social media performance.

PLANNED RTM: OTHER KNOWN EVENTS

Holidays are great and all, but savvy marketers know that there are far more opportunities each year to make a brand's voice heard. These smaller events are visible for months in advance, and while not fully commercialized, still create compelling and unique marketing opportunities. These are events that might not be on the radar for the majority of a brand's audience, but can resonate with a core group of followers that are die-hard fans of a certain subculture.

The opening day for a sports league, the conclusion to a popular television series, and other pop culture moments are just a few examples of topics that capture the attention of many for a short period of time, and will surely be the center of a huge amount of social conversation. If brands can see these events coming, and plan out a good real-time strategy to stay relevant with the audience, it can be a huge opportunity to boost social performance.

BREAKING BAD FINALE, 2013

In September 2013, worldwide audiences were excited and mourning at the same time. The time had come for one of the most talked-about shows on television, *Breaking Bad*, to come to an end after five seasons. Fans had loved watching Walter White turn more and more evil every week, and flocked to social media to express their joy, surprise, and excitement after every episode.

As the finale approached, brands were ready to stay relevant for their audience as well. While they are not a well-known, annual event like an awards show, series finales can give a huge ratings boost to a network. In this case, according to *Variety*, over ten million people watched the series play out in its final episode. This created a huge opportunity for brands to jump into the conversation, and they didn't disappoint.

Of the eight brands I saw comment on the *Breaking Bad* finale on Twitter (including Clorox, CoverGirl, Denny's, and Urban Outfitters), six of them saw a bump in their Twitter performance metrics versus their normal levels of activity. The average bump was significant, at 1,000 percent+ in retweets and 740 percent+ in favorites, but there was one brand that outweighed the rest in performance. Truvia, an artificial sweetener brand, jumped on a plot point in the finale to tweet a message to fans. I won't give it away for anyone who hasn't seen the end of the series, but it was on point and very relevant to the conversation happening the next morning. The performance was ridiculous—with an almost 7,500 percent bump in retweet performance and 5,000 percent bump in favorites.

This was a case of not only understanding that a large pop culture moment is happening but also jumping on a micro-event within the larger moment. Truvia didn't tweet about any of the regular subjects in the show, or give a goodbye kiss to the show via the #BreakingBad hashtag like a few other brands did. By being specific with their reference,

Figure 3.16 Tweet by the @Clorox team during the *Breaking Bad* finale in September 2013

they saw a huge bump in engagement and made the most of their real-time marketing moment.

STAR WARS DAY, 2014

There's a funky little day that has grown in popularity over the past few years among a somewhat geeky circle. It's May 4, or as is known in groups of people (like myself) who celebrate everything about *Star Wars*, "May the 4th Be with You Day." The event built its first official organized celebration in Toronto in 2011, and has been a popular topic for fans of the science fiction staple every year since, especially on social media. *Star Wars*, of course, has always been a popular subject for die-hard fans who can't wait to get their hands on the next film, video game, or novel that paints an exciting view of good versus evil using archetypal figures while transporting the audience into an entirely different universe. Plus, light sabers.

While *Star Wars* has been a phenomenon for decades, *Star Wars* day is relatively new to the pop culture landscape and therefore tends to sneak up on some people until the day itself. Many fans only finally realize it's May 4 when they see friends post about it on social networks. In 2014, it seemed, brands were ready.

In that year, brands were all over *Star Wars* Day on Twitter, and posted messages and media that they hoped would resonate with the day's micro-trend. Brands that ranged from NASA to Nissan to Delta Airlines (Figure 3.17) chimed in with funny and clearly Photoshopped media, using hashtags like "#MayThe4thBeWithYou" and "#HappyStarWarsDay" to keep the conversation going and gain more visibility with fans following the trend. It was amusing to watch from the sidelines, but did it provide a performance impact for these brands?

I pulled data for 20 brands that posted any manner of *Star Wars* Day real-time marketing on that Sunday, and compared the performance (retweets per follower and favorites per follower) to each brand's 2014 Twitter performance averages. The results were, shall we say, out of this world? (Boo, stop it.)

Figure 3.17 Delta's Tweet about *Star Wars* Day saw almost 100 percent more retweets and 75 percent+ more favorites than the brand's 2014 average Tweet performance

Of the 20 brands I ran the numbers for, 18 saw a performance bump (Figure 3.18). And that bump was pretty impressive. On average, the brands that I looked at saw a 360 percent+ increase in retweets and a 300 percent+ increase in favorites for their *Star Wars* Day-related content. Brands had created good creative that resonated with a real-time topic, and the audience responded accordingly. It's the same pattern we saw across all Trending Topic usage—far more brands seeing performance gains versus not, and the gains showing much more amplification versus any losses.

Some of the best examples, performance-wise, showcased solid creative that resonated with their audience:

Mountain Dew UK saw the biggest performance bump, with 1,600 percent+ more retweets and 1,000 percent+ more favorites versus

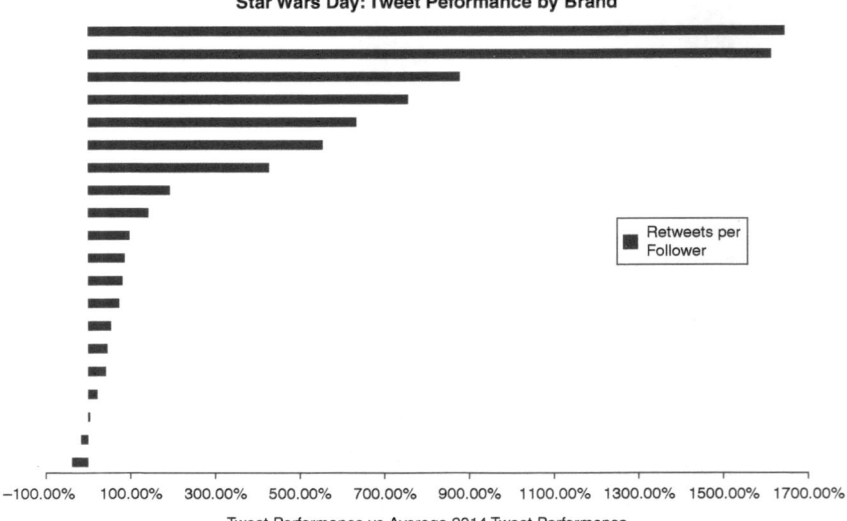

Figure 3.18 Retweet per follower performance, by brand, for RTM created about *Star Wars* Day 2014

their 2014 averages. The creative (Figure 3.19)—showing two different-sized bottles with Jedi capes on, was something the audience found to be extremely sharable and engaging.

Maker's Mark built out some clever copywriting skills and light saber-themed bourbon bottles (Figure 3.20) to see a huge bump in performance (800 percent+ increase in retweets and 500 percent+ bump in favorites versus the brand's 2014 average.) And as a side note, anytime I can include an example in a book about the combination of *Star Wars* and bourbon, well, let's just say that's going to happen every time.

Star Wars Day gave brands a unique opportunity—a known event that, to this point, had not been overcommercialized, and a topic that is highly relevant to a core group of fans who love anything to do with the subject matter. And as the numbers show, brands were rewarded for their work with increased engagement and sharing performance on Twitter.

Figure 3.19   Mountain Dew UK's *Star Wars* Day Tweet from May 4, 2014

GAME OF THRONES PREMIERE, SEASON 4

Over the past few years, *Game of Thrones* has become a pop culture phenomenon across the world. During each season, fans tune in to must-see appointment viewing and hang on every plot point as the story unfolds, one decapitated actor at a time. In April 2014, viewers

Figure 3.20   Maker's Mark's *Star Wars* Day Tweet, May 4, 2014

had been waiting months for the show's return, and on the day of the season premiere, brands of all sizes and shields knew there would be a concentration of attention around the subject of the show. Numerous brands and media companies jumped at the opportunity to make their messages and brand more relevant by joining the conversation that was already happening.

I tracked data from 15 different brands and media companies that posted *Game of Thrones*-related content on that Sunday, brands that included the NY Jets football franchise, Tim Horton's restaurant chain, Bud Light, and Pringles. I measured the sharing and engagement metrics that resulted from their RTM efforts, and compared it to each brand's normal levels of Twitter performance during 2014.

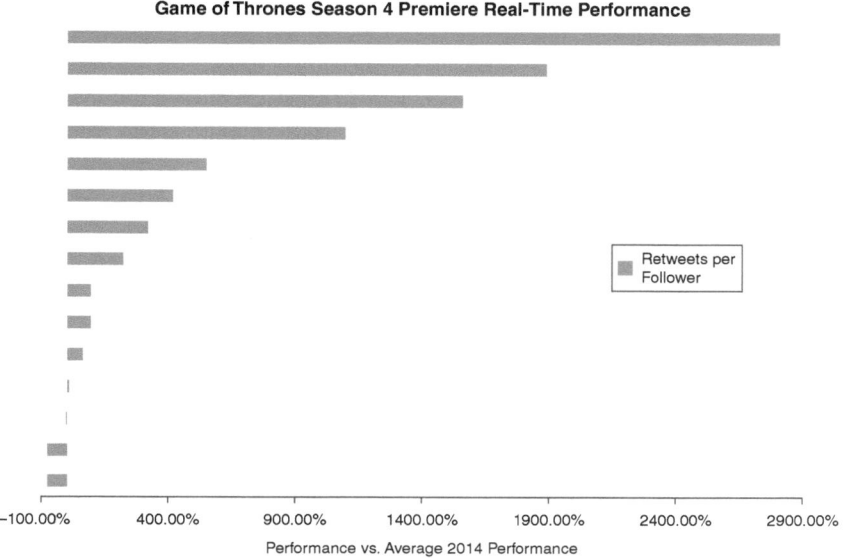

Figure 3.21 Retweet per follower performance, by brand, for RTM created around the *Game of Thrones* premiere, 2014

The marriage of timely content and a real-time medium produced great results. Brands, on average, saw close to a 600 percent bump in retweets and a 650 percent bump in favorites when compared to their normal social engagement levels from the same year (Figure 3.21). There were a few outliers that helped skew the average numbers higher, but 80 percent of brands saw an increase in their Tweet performance numbers by creating content around this trend. And as you can see from the distribution of performance, once again the positive results far outweighed the negative results realized by a few brands whose messages did not resonate with the audience.

Some of the positive stories from this campaign saw huge impacts to their social metrics. The Netflix series *House of Cards* smartly created content around the *Game of Thrones* premiere (Figure 3.22), keeping itself top of mind between seasons, and was rewarded with a 2,800 percent+ bump in retweets versus what they normally see. In addition, Clorox and Pringles saw 1,000 percent bumps from their *Game of Thrones* creative efforts.

House of Cards ✓
@HouseofCards   ✿   ·⚑ Follow

Welcome back, @GameofThrones. May the
best House win. #FU
pic.twitter.com/khWOHg3MXK

↰ Reply ⇄ Retweet ★ Favorite ••• More

LONG LIVE
THE KING

RETWEETS   FAVORITES
12,728   8,786

7:55 PM - 6 Apr 2014   Flag media

Figure 3.22 RTM Tweet from @HouseOfCards about the 2014 *Game of Thrones*
premiere

FOR MOST BIG EVENTS, RTM WORKS

Why did we just do this? Why did we just run about a thousand different analyses on real-time marketing data and its performance? Well,
there's been an ongoing debate in social that real-time marketing is
a flash in the pan and brings no real value. And I'm not necessarily
against those types of arguments, but I'd rather that people backed
it up with data. If you don't want to work during big events, I understand. If you think it's a bit odd to have a consumer packaged goods
brand tweeting during the Oscars about every little funny event that
happens, I get that it seems a bit weird and out of place at first. But in
a lot of scenarios, it really actually starts to make sense when you run
the numbers, and that's what I set out to investigate here.

　　We looked at the data to show that there are real impacts, across multiple brands and verticals, to engagement and social sharing on Twitter

for real-time marketing efforts over the past few years. Opportunistic RTM outperforms other social activities on Twitter pretty consistently— not just for one brand during one event, but for a high majority of brands over almost every event that we reviewed. We looked at the performance of social content that is prebaked but posted during tent-pole events, and while it outperforms the average social performance metrics, it comes nowhere close to the performance that RTM is seeing. And remember, you should use this as a guide for testing different tactics with your brand, not as gospel. Practices that work for one brand might not work for another, but these data points should help send you in the right direction for which types of tactics you can work into your social strategy to increase engagement.

We also saw, in the case of Planned RTM for big events and holidays, that simply including a Trending Topic around a known event doesn't guarantee success. It seems the audience is telling us that there are no free rides here. Your audience is smart, and the data is telling us that you need to work a bit harder for your performance. The audience, it seems, likes to be surprised.

But what we've been looking at here is big events. What about RTM for smaller events that pop up, and everyday trends that we can't see coming? That's what we'll tackle next.

This page intentionally left blank

Chapter 4

RTM PERFORMANCE FOR UNKNOWN EVENTS AND DAILY TRENDS

WE'VE SEEN HOW SOME OF THE LARGEST brands in the world are using Twitter, and we've seen how real-time marketing can deliver a measurable, consistent performance bump during tent-pole events. This is great to know when preparing for the Oscars or Grammys, but what do you do the other 360-odd days of the year? Before we answer that question, let's step back for a minute and talk about something completely different: that glorious sport known as baseball.

I've been a Seattle Mariners fan for over 20 years, and while the years have brought a Space Needle-sized portion of grief and losing seasons, they've also brought a few great players and moments along the way. My favorite player over the years, without a doubt, was number 51, Ichiro Suzuki, known in the baseball world as simply "Ichiro."

Ichiro is a unique breed of superstar. You see, in a sport where big moments dominate the headlines, Ichiro doesn't hit a lot of home runs. He doesn't swing for the fences each time he's up at the plate, trying to make a huge splash with every at bat. What Ichiro has done amazingly well over his career is *just get hits*. Everyday hits—singles that get him on base, time and time again. He has collected so many hits that in 2004 he set a single-season record when he recorded 262 of them. He takes this approach consistently, year over year, and is the only player in the history of baseball to get 200 hits in ten consecutive seasons. He's the personification of how lots of small successes can build and build and build into a giant advantage.

In today's social world, people are not just talking about big events that are planned out months in advance but also micro-trends that happen each and every day. With social media powering our new channels of communication, these short-lived but popular trends come and go faster than ever before. Topics are top of mind for hours instead of weeks, as the audience moves on to the next big thing.

So can a brand take advantage of these everyday trends to bring some of that attention back to them? Can they consistently show up every day to grab value, without necessarily having to make a big splash every time? Can they play the social game like Ichiro plays baseball, and if they do, will they see benefits in social media performance for their efforts?

In this chapter, we'll take a look at some everyday trends that appear on the right hand side of our RTM Matrix (Figure 4.1)—Watchlist trends that brands can *kind of* see coming, and Everyday trends that brands couldn't have planned for if they had tried—and see if joining in smaller trending topics results in social performance gains.

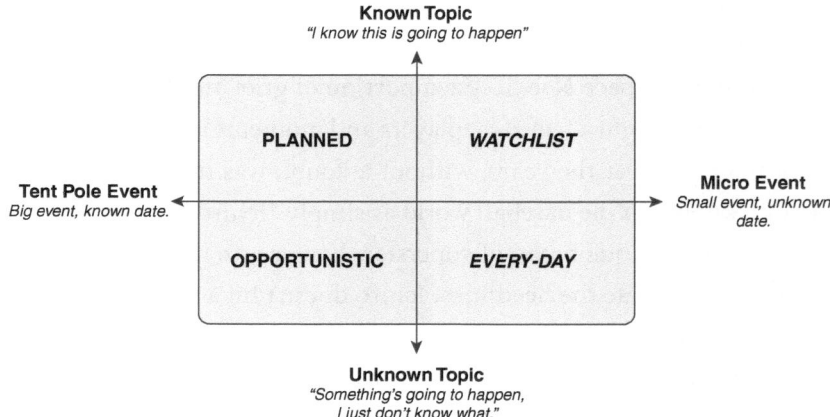

Figure 4.1   The RTM Matrix—Watchlist and Everyday Quadrants

WATCHLIST RTM

Uncertainty is part of the social media world, and with RTM it's no different. When you know an event is coming, but can't be sure of all the details, it takes a unique approach and a large dose of patience. Sometimes it can make you nervous, sometimes excited, and sometimes just downright frustrated. But in the world of real-time marketing, it's a feeling that brands should start getting used to.

In the upper right quadrant of our matrix lies Watchlist RTM, which I affectionately referred to earlier in this book as "The Bieber Quadrant." You know something's going to happen around a certain topic, but you don't know exactly when or exactly what. And not only that, you also know that when something does happen, the world (or at least your audience) will take notice, and the conversation of the day should turn to that subject. If a brand can do careful planning and foresee Watchlist RTM topics, they can be ready with solid creative when something finally happens.

But knowing that the world will be talking about a certain subject does a brand no good if the audience doesn't care that the brand is along for the ride. So when it comes to Watchlist RTM content, how does the audience respond?

I found a number of examples from the past year of multiple brands creating RTM around Watchlist events to capitalize on relevant topics for their audience. Some of these examples might surprise you, and others might seem out of bounds for a brand, but we'll see how each performed with engagement and sharing metrics on Twitter. Let's start in jolly old England.

THE ROYAL BABY

On December 3, 2012, it was announced that the Duchess of Cambridge was expecting her first child. For the next seven months, the entire globe was abuzz with excitement and speculation about all things Royal Baby. On July 22, 2013, the Duchess gave birth to a boy weighing 8 pounds, 6 ounces at St. Mary's Hospital in Paddington, and His Royal Highness Prince George of Cambridge joined the royal family as its newest member. Twitter, in analytics terms, went nutso.

In the next 48 hours, the #RoyalBaby hashtag would be included in over 600,000 Tweets, in addition to large amounts of chatter about the parents and Prince George himself. As celebrities and commoners alike shared their excitement via social media, brands saw a chance to jump in on the conversation now that the event had finally arrived.

I pulled Twitter data for 13 brands that posted #RoyalBaby-themed content that week, and saw some impressive performance. On average, brands saw a 1,200 percent+ bump in retweets per follower, and a 940 percent+ bump in favorites per follower by using relevant Royal Baby content in their Tweets that week. But as you could probably guess by now, it didn't just work for one brand. It worked for a whole lot of them. As you can see in Figure 4.3, twelve of the thirteen brands I looked at saw a higher-than-normal retweets per follower performance bump with their Royal Baby RTM.

Figure 4.2   RTM tweet from @Hostess_Snacks about the birth of the Royal Baby, July 2013

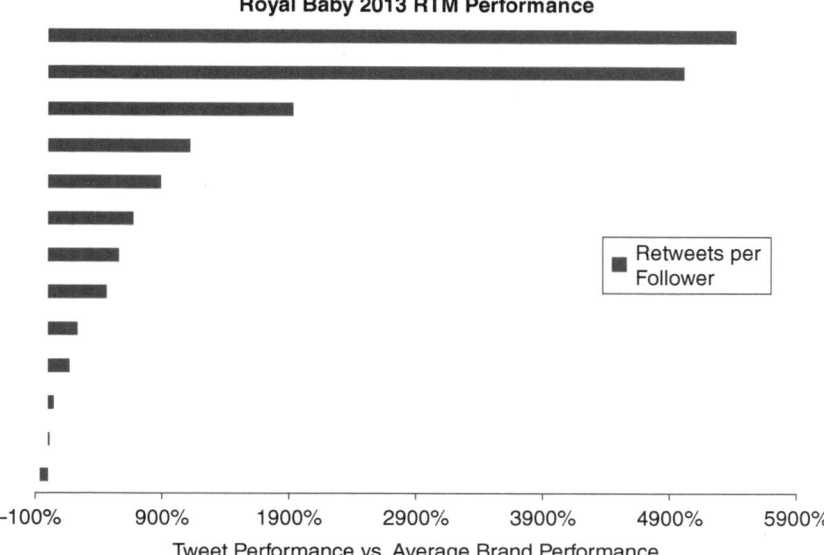

Figure 4.3 Retweet per Follower performance, by brand, for RTM created around the birth of the Royal Baby, July 2013

Alongside the Royal Baby RTM were a good number of articles and Tweets poking fun at brands for creating this content. Much of the content was labeled as dull and irrelevant by critics, who called the overall brand response to the birth a failure. I can agree that a few of the creative efforts didn't strike me as clever or revolutionary, but the timing of the content created amazing gains for the majority of brands that participated. What looks silly to some might make more sense when they see the performance numbers.

IN MEMORIAM

From time to time, our society loses someone who has had such a wide-reaching impact on our daily lives that it makes the entire world stop to take a breath. A few of those moments happened in 2013 and 2014.

On December 5, 2013, Nelson Mandela passed away at his home in Johannesburg, South Africa. He had spent decades sharing his message of peace and justice, and the world mourned his passing in print, on television, and on social networks. News outlets tweeted breaking news about his death and past reminders about the breadth of his legacy. Politicians and other influential individuals took to social networks to share their grief and celebrate Mandela's life with their followers. Celebrities tweeted brief stories and told of the impact Mandela had made on their lives.

On the morning of May 28, 2014, Maya Angelou passed away. She had led a long life as a creative visionary, as a world-renowned author and a poet. She, too, was honored by influential people from all different backgrounds that day as artifacts from her poetry, essays, and interviews flooded the Internet in tribute to her great life and impact on society. Tweets containing text quotes or images with her wise words flooded newsfeeds around the world.

In both cases, individuals weren't the only ones showing their respect to the late great visionaries. Brands joined the conversation and celebrated the lives of both with their followers.

Figure 4.4   RTM Tweet by @BananaRepublic memorializing Maya Angelou, May 2014

For Nelson Mandela's passing, I saw ten different brands create Tweets that memorialized the great leader. These weren't news organizations just posting breaking news alerts; rather, brands like Starbucks, Cisco, Ralph Lauren, and eBay created polished, respectful content around the topic. For Maya Angelou's passing, I also found ten brands that posted Twitter content spreading her message and wishing for her to rest in peace. Brands like Nordstrom, Banana Republic, Benefit Beauty, and Audible.com took the day off from sending out offers and tweeted their own tributes to her.

The audience responded extremely favorably, with an average 600 percent+ retweets per follower rate and almost a 500 percent+ favorites per follower rate versus each brand's normal levels. And the distribution of success over the 20 brands in the combined list (Figure 4.5) follows our same familiar pattern that we've seen before—95 percent of brands saw an increase over normal levels of engagement and sharing.

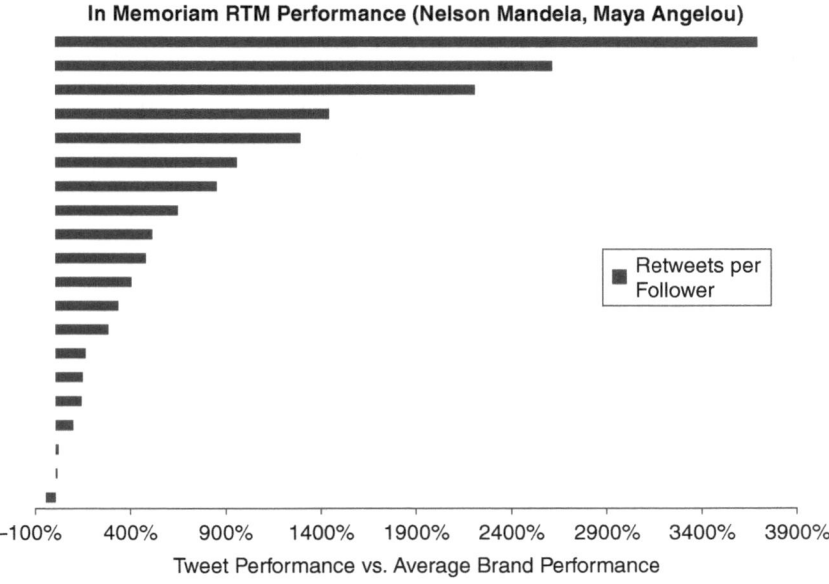

Figure 4.5 Combined data sets for retweet-per-follower performance, by brand, for RTM created about the passing of Nelson Mandela and Maya Angelou

Now this category is one that makes it a bit difficult to celebrate a performance bump in social metrics. It's a delicate subject, and one that brands will all take a different stance on. I'm certainly not one to preach and dictate what a brand should or shouldn't do with its own voice and messaging. That being said, it's difficult to recommend that a brand create in-memoriam social content due to social media performance bumps. That's a bit much for my pay grade.

What I will say is this: if your brand wants to create a genuine in-memoriam message when a popular figure passes away, but are concerned that the audience won't be there with you, this data should encourage you to do so, and there's a good chance the audience will respond favorably. On the other hand, if you're looking to create social content around the passing of a well-recognized figure *just* to get a social performance bump, you may want to reconsider.

RTM AND OTHER BREAKING NEWS

We've walked through a number of examples in which brands have managed to work their way into a diverse set of trending conversations. Some of the trends make perfect sense for a brand to have an opinion on—for example, when the topic matches the goods and services a particular brand sells, or echoes the message from a brand's current ad campaign. But some brands have started to become more vocal on other subjects—more controversial ones—and are seeing a big response from the audience for stepping into the spotlight on one side of an issue.

No matter where you stand on whether a brand should chime in on a political issue, it's happening. And my big question is, of course, how does the audience respond? Is the message ignored as an unwelcome visitor to a personal conversation, or as brands become more personified and approachable, are these tactics engaging their audiences with relevant content? Let's look at a few examples.

Brands Chime in on Marriage Equality

The Virgin brand has never been a quiet one, and Twitter seems like a perfect medium for the brand to connect with its hip, sophisticated target demographic. The brand's keeper, Sir Richard Branson, has always been an outspoken advocate of many political issues, and in fact announced in 2006 that all Virgin Holiday profits in the foreseeable future would be donated to research for developing sustainable sources of energy.

After Parliament passed a major milestone for a same-sex marriage bill in February 2013, Virgin decided to voice its opinion on the matter via Twitter (Figure 4.6), and give a subtle hint at its own product offerings at the same time. The response was impressive.

Follower responses led to a huge increase in levels of engagement and sharing compared to what Virgin Holiday's Twitter content normally experiences. The Tweet received a 5,000 percent bump in retweets per

Figure 4.6 RTM Tweet from @VirginHolidays on the subject of a same sex marriage bill passing in Parliament

follower and a 1,200 percent+ bump in favorites per follower versus the brand's average levels.

In the United States, a few brands did the same when the US Supreme Court struck down the Defense of Marriage Act as unconstitutional in June 2013. One of those was Marc Jacobs International, a clothing brand and retailer that decided to voice an opinion via social media.

The Tweet from @MarcJacobsIntl (Figure 4.7) received a 710 percent+ bump in retweets per follower and a 312 percent+ increase in favorites per follower versus the brand's other Twitter content.

Both brands, among many others, decided to voice an opinion on a controversial subject, and by jumping on a relevant topic and providing a genuine message of support, that move turned into a social marketing win.

Figure 4.7 RTM Tweet from @MarcJacobsIntl celebrating the Supreme Court DOMA ruling, June 2013

Ben & Jerry's Meets Colorado

Oh, Ben & Jerry's. Who doesn't love a company that not only creates wonderful super-premium ice cream flavors that taste delightful but also delights you with their unique naming conventions? For years we've enjoyed "Cherry Garcia," "Chubby Hubby," Stephen Colbert's "Americone Dream," and now even the new "That's My Jam" Jam-infused ice cream. Is anyone else getting hungry?

Anyway, when the state of Colorado passed Amendment 64, a referendum supporting the legalization of marijuana, Ben & Jerry's jumped on the still-controversial subject to chime in with a clever and effective Tweet. Can you guess which side the maker of an ice cream flavor called "Hazed and Confused" came down on the legalization vote?

Ben and Jerry's Tweet (Figure 4.8), which included an image of an empty ice cream store shelf, received results better than any other social content they created in the first half of 2014, garnering an almost 6,000 percent boost in retweets per follower and an almost 3,000 percent

Figure 4.8   RTM Tweet from @benandjerrys on the topic of Colorado's passing of Amendment 64

bump in favorites per follower. Ben & Jerry's, by jumping on a breaking news story in the moment and building out a funny take on the subject, created content that resonated with what was top of mind for the audience in the moment.

EVERYDAY RTM

Every hour new trends appear on Twitter—and disappear hours later. But during the brief period that they are popular, these micro-trends can still bring large amounts of attention that brands can take advantage of. It's the new reality for each brand's audience—attention is increasingly scattered, and the topics that will be important and trending tomorrow are even more unpredictable than the day before. It's up to brands to quickly identify, execute on, and analyze their performance for these unknown daily trends. The results can be impressive.

How fast are these trends moving? Let's take an average day, in this case March 1, 2014, and see what happened across Twitter.

- In the United States, there were 400+ distinct Twitter Trending Topics.
- In New York City, there were 130+ distinct Twitter Trending Topics.
- At the worldwide level, there were 1,500+ distinct Twitter Trending Topics.
- The term with the widest trending reach, #CamAndNashNew Video, trended in 65 locations across the globe.
- It also happened to be Justin Bieber's birthday (I had no idea when I picked this date, I swear), spawning multiple hashtags across the globe about his big day.

And "Mardi Gras." And #Hannibal. And IHOP, #Scandal, "March Madness," "Allen Iverson," #NASCAR, and tons more.

Wow, that's a lot going on. And given that social media teams have day jobs, keeping an eye on these fast-moving trends seems almost impossible. As a brand, how do you even choose the right one? And once you identify the right one, jump on, and post content about a Trending Topic, who's to say it will still be a thing? Why would brands want to go to all this trouble in the first place? If these trends come and go so fast, can it even be worth the effort of jumping on an everyday Trending Topic to capture some of the audience's attention?

So, first of all, you're starting to sound like an old person. That's ok—I'm an old person, too (at least in the start-up world), and when I first saw brands jumping on everyday Trending Topics, I assumed it was a fad that would quickly die out, and we could all go back to business as it's always been, with business casual attire and everyone always filling out their TPS reports on time. But then I started to look at the numbers.

Let's look at this practice from a performance perspective and see if we can learn what some of these brands might already know. As we saw earlier when we look across our 100+ brands, we see an average 99 percent bump in retweets per follower and an 81 percent bump in favorites per follower when brands use an everyday Trending Topic in their Twitter content. We also saw the distribution of performance, showing that this practice, on average, works for almost 70 percent of the brands that use it. But let's see if we can get even more specific than that and walk through some Trending Topic hashtags to see how brands chime in, and what the performance looks like per topic.

We'll use some of the brands from our 100+ data set for this next set of analyses, but we'll need to grab data for a few more brands for each Trending Topic that we're interested in. We'll look at the performance of four everyday Trending Topics that saw brand participation during the month of May 2014, and see what the data tells us. The next time you see a clever hashtag trending, should you get your brand involved? Let's see.

TRENDING TOPIC 1: #RUINARAPTRACK

On May 5, 2014, a Comedy Central show created a hashtag that got their viewers, and brands, talking on Twitter. The game show, named *Midnight* and hosted by Chris Hardwick, asked the contestants and the audience to try their hand at creating terrible music during a segment called "#HashtagWars." The prompt was to make a hip-hop song worse by changing a few of the lyrics, with the hashtag of the night being "#RuinARapTrack."

The contestants gave their answers, many of which I can't repeat in this book, and the show rolled on. But through the power of social media, the segment's impact on pop culture didn't stop there. The audience at home kept rolling with their answers on Twitter throughout the night and into the next day. And as the hashtag began to trend across the United States, brands began jumping on board.

Now, sure, if you're new to social media you might wonder why on earth a brand like Crest, as we see in Figure 4.9, would be changing rap lyrics and tweeting them out to their fans. Crest is a toothpaste brand, after all, and the last time I checked, there's not a big crossover between hip-hop and fluoride. I hear you loud and clear. What we are seeing here is that even if it seems weird to see a brand chiming in on a micro-trend, it works with today's social audience to boost engagement and virality. And it doesn't just work for a few brands. It turns out it works for most of them. In fact, of the ten brands that jumped on the #RuinARapTrack trend (Figure 4.10), only two received lower than average engagement and share rates with their followers versus each brand's other Twitter content in 2014.

Figure 4.9   Crest's #RunARapTrack Tweet earned the brand a 2,000 percent+ higher retweets and 3,000 percent+ higher favorites versus their other Twitter content in 2014

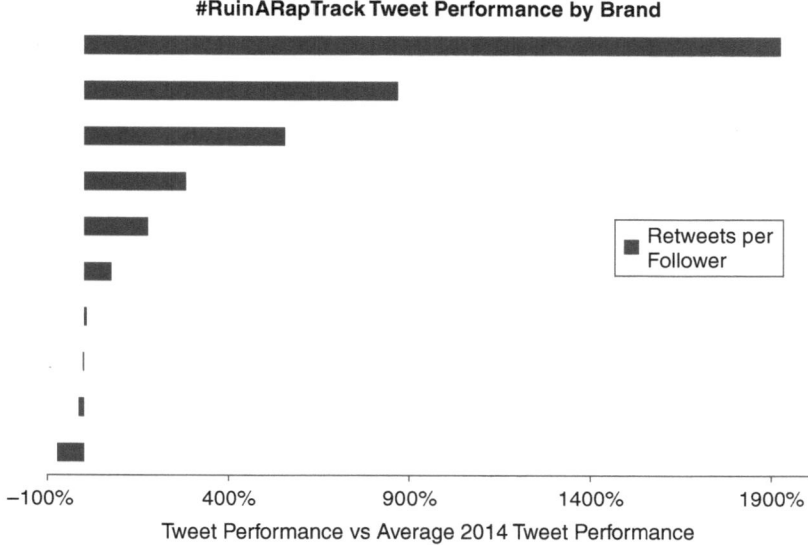

Figure 4.10   Retweet-per-follower performance, by brand, for RTM created around the #RuinARapTrack Twitter Trending Topic

Not only did these Tweets perform better but they performed *a lot better*—the average Tweet showed a 380 percent bump in retweets and a 350 percent+ bump in favorites versus their average performance over the past few months. We're seeing the same pattern here that we've seen many times before in this book—relevant content drives a huge amount of upside and a small amount of downside for participating brands.

TRENDING TOPIC 2: #UNDATEABLEBECAUSE

On May 21, 2014, the hashtag "#UndateableBecause" began trending across the United States, with Twitter users chiming in with amusing reasons why their potential mates might be out of their personal consideration, including not liking video games, refusing to eat their favorite food, and even some more serious responses. In the span of only a few hours, the hashtag saw tens of thousands of mentions, and then a few smart brands that noticed the trend started to chime in as well.

Figure 4.11 RTM Tweet from @panerabread including the #UndateableBecause Twitter Trending Topic

Panera Bread

When Panera crafted a quick Tweet (Figure 4.11) combining the Trending Topic and plugging their Cheddar Broccoli Soup, the audience reacted with tremendous enthusiasm. The Tweet saw a 200 percent+ bump in retweets per follower and a 50 percent bump in favorites per follower compared to their 2014 averages.

NissanUSA

Nissan also took a simple approach to plugging their newest 370Z vehicle and received a big performance bump, thanks to the trend. Their Tweet (Figure 4.12) received a 40 percent+ increase in retweets per follower and a 100 percent bump in favorites per follower versus averages for the year.

This trend was not planned in advance or visible on any editorial calendar, but brands that had built a system to quickly identify, create ideas, and post social content received a bump in their social metrics for their efforts. What may seem strange to someone first seeing this practice—what does Nissan have to do with dating advice?—has become the norm for many brands across the globe. Brands are chiming in on conversations that are already happening and seeing performance bumps from hyperrelevant content created in the moment.

Degrassi

The Twitter account for Degrassi, a Canadian show that airs on MTV and TeenNick, also jumped on the #UndateableBecause hashtag and

Figure 4.12   RTM Tweet from @NissanUSA including the #UndateableBecause
Twitter Trending Topic

Figure 4.13   RTM Tweet from @Degrassi

found that the topic resonated with their audience. Not surprisingly, dating seems to be top of mind for Degrassi's younger demographic, and the Tweet (Figure 4.13) received a 65 percent bump in retweets per follower and a 110 percent+ increase to favorites per follower versus their average 2014 Twitter performance.

TRENDING TOPIC 3: #CAPSLOCKDAY

On May 23, 2014, it was proclaimed "ALL CAPS DAY" to celebrate the practice of "Internet shouting" across Twitter. The topic trended across the United States, and brands began to jump in to offer funny and sometimes insightful commentary on the micro-event.

Of the eight brands I saw jump in on the trend, five saw a performance bump in their Tweet performance when compared to each brand's historical numbers. Here are a few examples of good content that not only entertained but also performed:

Verizon FiOS

Verizon's FiOS account jumped in on the trend (Figure 4.14) with an *Anchorman* quote (which a few other brands used as well), and saw enormous amounts of engagement and sharing from their followers. Verizon enjoyed a 1,800 percent+ bump in retweets per follower and a 700 percent+ favorites per follower.

USA TODAY

The news hub's #CAPSLOCKDAY Tweet, seen in Figure 4.15, was not only informative as to the origins of the term "upper case" but it was also shared and favorited heavily by the audience. The Tweet received 250 percent+ more retweets per follower and almost 300 percent more

Figure 4.14 Tweet from @VerizonFIOS including the #CAPSLOCKDAY Twitter Trending Topic

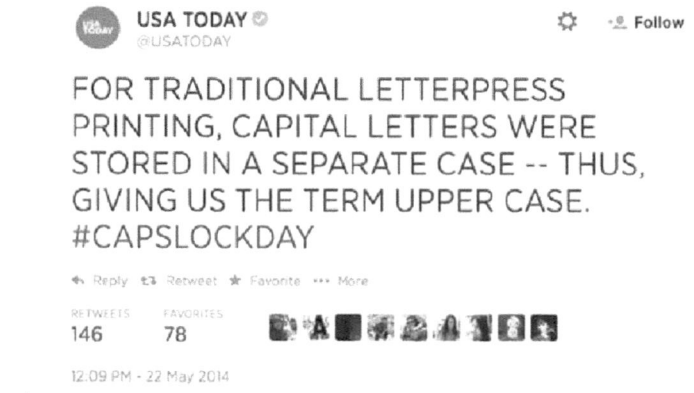

Figure 4.15   Tweet from @USATODAY including the #CAPSLOCKDAY Twitter
Trending Topic

favorites per follower than their historical average for original social
content. Nicely done.

Micro-trends come and go, and their connection to a brand might be
small to none, but that doesn't mean brands can't jump in on the right
trend that resonates with the crowd, especially if that communication is
happening in the very channel where the trend is taking place. Because
these smart marketers jumped on an everyday Trending Topic in the
moment and responded on the right channel, they were able to make
their brand relevant to the moment and followers responded with big
numbers.

TRENDING TOPIC 4: #YOUWERECUTEUNTIL

On May 27, 2014, the hashtag "#YouWereCuteUntil" began trending on
Twitter across the United States. It's an example of how an unknown
trend that didn't exist 48 hours before, thanks to the power and pace of
social media, can quickly become a worldwide Trending Topic. Twitter
users jumped on the trend to share their turnoffs (over 110,000 Tweets
within the two-day time period), and brands quickly joined the everyday Trending Topic to tell their own story.

I tracked the performance of ten brands that used the hashtag in a Tweet that day, and saw impressive performance gains from the group. Eight of the ten brands using the hashtag saw a performance bump versus their Tweet performance from the rest of 2014, with an average 428 percent increase in retweets per follower. Nine of the ten brands saw a bump in favorites per follower versus their 2014 levels of engagement, with the average brand seeing a 280 percent increase in favorites per follower.

Brands like the Montreal Canadiens hockey team (1,300 percent+ increase to retweets per follower), CMT (1,200 percent+ bump to retweets per follower) and Waffle House (650 percent increase in retweets per follower) all saw impressive social sharing thanks to their understanding of the importance in creating relevant content in the moment.

As we look at the distribution of performance (Figure 4.16), we see a shape that should be looking familiar by now.

Once again, the reward is worth the risk for brands jumping in on a Trending Topic hashtag. More brands are seeing increases versus decreases in performance, and the positives far outweigh any negative impact that brands experience. The RTM Wave continues to roll.

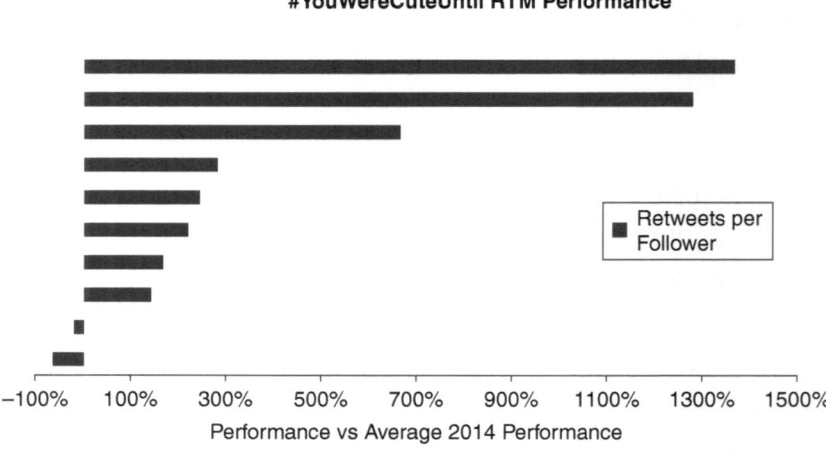

#YouWereCuteUntil RTM Performance

Retweets per Follower

Performance vs Average 2014 Performance

Figure 4.16 Retweet-per-follower performance, by brand, for brand tweets including the #YouWereCuteUntil hashtag

And again, all four of these Trending Topics had nothing to do with the brands that chimed in. These weren't auto companies jumping on a #roadtrip hashtag, or the NBA commenting on a #NBADraft topic. These were generic, nondenominational conversations happening on Twitter that brands had to identify, brainstorm, and create content for on the fly. Critics might still say this practice is odd and doesn't make any sense for a brand, but it works.

THERE'S REAL VALUE IN THE EVERYDAY

So what can we take away from all of this? It seems that the pattern that we saw around big, known events is carrying over into the smaller ones as well. Even if it's strange to see a brand chiming in on a breaking news subject that has nothing to do with its business model, or watching a brand flex its rap muscles for the audience as part of its daily routine, the practice works. It works really, really well.

Why does it work? Well, as brands become more connected with their consumers, this shift just makes sense. Today's consumer seems to find it easier to connect to a brand that has a voice, and isn't afraid to use it. You can't have a conversation with someone who never takes a chance or has no core set of beliefs that he or she wants to express. You can't have a conversation with someone who isn't talking about what you're interested in, and is always changing the subject to his or her own agenda. Or, I guess I should say—you *can* have a conversation with that person, but it won't be a *long conversation*.

What we've learned about RTM over the past two chapters is pretty clear—when brands engage in most forms of RTM, followers respond with enthusiasm. If you're in charge of your brand's social media efforts and driving these types of social KPIs are important to you, then building out an RTM program should have just made your short list for the next few months. And if your boss is reading this book, you should already have a plan in place when he or she asks you tomorrow morning what your plans are for jumping on daily trends. Don't have a plan in place? That's ok—that's where we are heading next.

Now that we have some data in our back pocket, we'll dive into building out a real-time marketing program. And not just any RTM program. No, no, my friend. We're talking about a data-driven real-time marketing program. You see, not only can we use data to demonstrate that RTM outperforms other social efforts on Twitter, we can also use data in every step of the process. Because without data, RTM can be chaos. And nobody likes chaos, at least no one who's employable. We'll use data to figure out the best tactics to use, how to staff our RTM team, how to measure performance, and how to learn from the competition. With data on your side, you'll be more confident and better looking. Or at least more confident.

Chapter 5

LAYING A DATA-DRIVEN FOUNDATION FOR REAL-TIME

WE'VE LOOKED AT THE DATA AROUND real-time, and keep seeing that brands acting in the moment are enjoying a huge response from the audience. Real-time marketing efforts, as we've measured on Twitter, receive a great response from followers across multiple success metrics. This stuff isn't only an interesting way for a brand to stand out and become more human, more fun, more interesting—it actually works to promote higher levels of engagement and social sharing with the fan base. We don't need to rely just on the opinions of marketers to hear their thoughts on RTM—if it's silly or important or ridiculous— now that we've got data that shows its effectiveness.

These new findings answer some questions but create many new ones. What's the best way for a brand to approach RTM? Should my brand get involved, and if so, what's the best way to begin? How can I build a real-time marketing process that performs?

While data shows that RTM can make sense for brands, it doesn't remove the need for a strong framework to do real-time effectively. We shouldn't just be using data to look at past efforts and see how they performed. We should be using it at every step to make our real-time tactics smarter. Over the next few chapters, we're going to walk through a data-driven methodology and approach to RTM that helps turn what could be the craziest thing you do all year into something that's goal oriented, well researched, and positioned for social success.

Wait a minute, I can hear you saying, putting structure and process around RTM will make it boring. It will destroy the very shoot-from-the-hip mind-set that makes real-time effective. I didn't get into the social media business to have a predictable job. I got into this because I never know what's coming the next day. There's no data, no plan, and that's what makes it fun. What are you doing? This is boring. You're ruining *everything*.

Believe it or not, adding process to your real-time efforts will actually increase your ability to generate good ideas, to communicate with your fans on the fly, to be funnier or more insightful or whatever it is your brand is aiming for. A predictable framework can boost creativity. A solid methodology behind the scenes can help you to be proclaimed "the social media winner" the next day due to your genius, at least what will appear to be genius to the outside world. How did they think of that so fast? How did they know that would work so well? What they don't see is the planning, research, and execution that rely on solid data and insights to build up to that moment.

And still, even if we tried to make RTM a boring exercise by using a framework, it would be impossible to remove all the adrenaline from the process. Luckily for you thrill-seekers out there, I'll give you some great news: data isn't going to solve all your problems when it comes to RTM. With all of the variability in any live event, I can assure you that if you're engaged in real-time marketing, you're still going to get your share of curve balls. No doubt. A good methodology isn't going to keep Miley Cyrus's clothes on or prevent Matthew McConaughey from speaking his mind when he accepts an award. Guaranteed.

What a good data-driven methodology can do is get you prepared. It's going to give you guardrails. It's going to give you a good, go-to process to rely on when something crazy happens. You'll be able to control the chaos and take full advantage of the opportunity. You'll see opportunities that your competition doesn't see, and avoid land mines that they might not see coming. Your team will know what's in bounds and out of bounds, and won't waste cycles on ideas that would never make it to execution.

You see, RTM without a good methodology behind it is *crazytown*. And RTM with a good, data-driven approach is a *controlled slide*.

There are still a lot of thrills in the moment, and you can still make some big waves. But you'll be able to sleep the night before, knowing you're ready. And what's more comforting than nice, warm data? So in this chapter, we'll set the stage with a solid foundation to help you insure that you're ready to go, and have metrics and business intelligence on your side for all your RTM efforts.

METHODOLOGIES AREN'T BAD THINGS

I can hear you: "Oh no—let's not build a methodology. That sounds painful. Please don't do this… you seemed so nice."

Yes, a methodology. We're going to be building out a process that your team can walk through to prepare for every big event, every upcoming campaign, and building out everyday real-time marketing as well. Once you learn the steps, and how to bring data into your social efforts, it will become second nature. You'll wonder how you ever got along without it. It will be a good friend—telling you things you need to know, keeping you in check when you step out of line, and giving you all the information your team needs to make the right decisions.

Methodologies and process get a bad rap, and I get it. I hate being forced into a process more than anyone else, especially one that makes no sense and includes a bunch of steps you have to take because it's always been done that way. Well, luckily we can think of this methodology a little differently. It's not something that you're being forced to do—it's something you'll want to do. You'll get better returns if you do your homework up front, have a solid RTM team in place, set goals, and execute with confidence. These steps will help you do your job better or learn how others do their social jobs well. You'll make it look easy, while still doing the hard work behind the scenes. You'll learn that if brands are doing social well, they are displaying the trait of the mighty duck—the duck that, while looking peaceful and serene and happy floating gracefully on the water's surface, is actually pedaling like hell underneath the water to get where he needs to go. You're going to be that duck—with a lot of work going on in the background to produce a great, well-polished real-time marketing effort. I don't want to be a duck, you say. Well, too bad—because ducks get promoted.

Ok, enough with the metaphors. Let's keep this train chugging along. Damn, there I go again.

DATA AND CREATIVE, WORKING TOGETHER

Over the past few years, teams have realized that the combination of data and creative can bring great results if they are used in the right way. But the key is to keep the following in mind: data is not a replacement for creativity, and vice versa. You can optimize and A/B test and measure all day long—but if you don't have good, strong creative concepts out of the gate, you're never going to get anywhere. I've never seen a clever and effective ad campaign created completely via algorithm, and I'm pretty sure the only person who would like to see one is another algorithm. And on the other side, creative efforts need to be grounded in reality. Campaigns need goals and measurements to figure out what worked and didn't work, and hopefully gain insight into why things turned out the way they did.

So let's be clear—by laying out a data-driven approach to real-time marketing, I'm not saying that data rules over all. What's important to know is that each practice has its place and its own yard and its own ownership. We can make creative decisions that aren't supported by data, but it's best to do that when we have all the information that we can get. Then we say, "We're going in this direction, even though the data points to something else, and we're making this trade-off because of X and Y and Z." That's a fine approach, and a reasonable approach. It's not a creative lead storming out of a meeting because the quants have taken over, and it's not an analyst thinking they are better than an art director because they know how to build a pivot table. Everybody calm down. We're all going to work together on this one, and we'll get better results because of it.

Great, so where do we start?

We're going to start by looking at real-time marketing from an objective position. We're in the trust tree now—we can be honest and open with each other. We're going to talk about how to lay down a solid foundation for RTM. This stuff doesn't just show up on a Twitter feed via magic; rather, it takes a lot of work not only on your social team but throughout the organization.

BECOMING A REAL-TIME BRAND

To become a brand that functions in real-time and become relevant to your audience, you need more than just a social media staffer with a quick wit and access to your Twitter account's password—you need an entire system built out around you. Your social team needs to be able to act, know how to act, and know they are free to be creative and responsive. To build this capability out from an organizational standpoint, that means resources, executive support, budget, and authority.

You'll get the most out of real-time marketing when you have the support of every key area of your organization. If you have a CEO who reads an article on this week's latest RTM victory and proclaims that your brand must do the same, but demands to personally approve every Facebook post that goes on your brand's page, well, that's not going to work out so well (and if you happen to be that CEO and you're reading this book now, please stop doing that). So I want us not only to be realistic about the ability to change an entire organization overnight but also to understand that companies can change and that you can help be that change agent. And we'll talk about how to use the best change agent out there: data. First, let's get started by assessing your current organization.

EXECUTIVE SUPPORT

An RTM team with support from the C-Level is a successful team.

This may be the most important trait of a brand that's ready to step into the real-time world, due to the fact that many of the other success factors follow this one critical step. Getting an executive sponsor on board to support your RTM efforts helps pave the way for success, from resources to PR support to having a long-term view for success from the top down (and not pulling the plug after one event.)

RESOURCES

A well-stocked RTM team is a successful team.

Do you have a great, cross-functional social team? Do you have a dedicated real-time marketing group that has time to plan, educate themselves, execute, and analyze after a big event? Have you carved out a dedicated RTM budget? If social has been made a priority in your company, then you're probably off to a good start in this department. I recommend you expand the scope of your RTM team to include a cross-functional group that not only creates content but also empowers the team to act. You don't want everyone in your company and their mother trying to do real-time marketing. Instead, you need a set of solid performers who know what they're doing.

AUTHORITY

An RTM team that has been given the authority to act is a successful team.

Nothing, and I mean nothing, is worse than having a great, timely idea to post on social media, and then running into a two-day approval cycle. Sorry, we can't post that because of the wording. Give me a few hours, because I need to run this through legal. Meanwhile, all the other RTM brands are running around social networks like free spirits, dancing to a sweet Grateful Dead bootleg from 1976, tweeting at will, and getting great performance bumps for their efforts. If you're an RTM brand and you're going to participate in the moment, you need the authority to act and turn on a dime. Unfortunately, we live in a world where trends have a short shelf life, and if you have a long approval process from creative, legal, executives, or whoever, you'll miss out on chiming in as the world turns its attention to the next big thing. In fact, you could actually do harm to your brand by chiming in on day-old trends, showing off the fact that you can't be nimble in a nimble world. But there are ways around this, and we'll address this with our methodology and team structure.

RISK MEETS REWARD

Well, I can hear you saying—those are three great things to have but, unfortunately, I don't have any of them. Looks like I won't be jumping on this real-time boat after all. Do you guys validate or should I just…

Nothing is set in stone. Your brand might not turn on a dime today, or have the right processes or team in place at the current moment, but let's not give up quite yet. Think about it from the perspective of your leadership team—their brand is a valuable thing, and they want to protect it.

When I was in business school, the program did a great job of building our understanding of how a business works from multiple angles and viewpoints. From accounting to strategy to economics to marketing, we were taught about every in and out of modern-day business and how to use each to our advantage in our careers. But there was a moment about halfway through the program that taught me a lot about not only businesses but also how people running some of the biggest businesses in the world think.

One day at the start of class, one of my favorite professors kicked off his lecture by asking a very simple question: "Why are we doing this? What is the biggest thing we are here to teach you as you get your MBA?"

The answers came, with topics that you could probably predict. "To maximize shareholder value." That wasn't the answer he was looking for. "To create a greater good for humanity and give something back." Wrong. "To make the most money possible." Nice try.

And so on and so on. Nobody got it right. And after a few minutes, he finally revealed the simple truth that no one had guessed. What was his answer?

"To manage risk. We are here to teach you how to manage risk and balance it with reward."

Not only were we all wrong but it was an eye-opener for the class as to why businesses, especially older and more established businesses, do what they do. It's not all just about getting as much revenue as possible. It's about keeping the unknowns in check. It's about protecting the market share you already have. There are plenty of companies that earn the headlines of the *New York Times* and *Wired* magazine for making huge bets with unproven strategies, but there are also plenty of companies that just don't do that at all.

Now, add social media to that equation. For an older, established company, social media can look like a hornet's nest of risk. It's what lawyers see when they look up "risk" in their corporate dictionaries. In many executives' minds, it's an unpredictable, wild, bucking stallion and it will *not* be invited back to the holiday party next year if it keeps behaving like that. And then add real-time marketing to the mix—social media performed with split-second response times—and woo-boy, you're really just asking for it at that point.

We're not going to change how business leaders think overnight, so we might as well play by the same set of rules. And knowing what we now know about many leaders' adversity to risk, there are two ways we can help change hearts and minds.

The first is to reduce the risk. The second is to show the reward that comes along with the risk. And when we do that, then we'll be speaking the same language as your executive team.

REDUCING THE RISK

For brands, risk is about the unknown. With any venture that a brand decides to take on, there will be the upside and the possible downsides— lost revenue, damaging the public's perception of a brand, opening the door for competition, legal issues, and much, much more. Risk can take down a big brand if not managed properly, or avoided altogether. Risk is what keeps the CEO up at night.

And, let's be honest, social media is full of these types of situations. Giving your audience a public forum to air their grievances, essentially handing the keys to your brand over to a few social media people at your company or agency, chiming in on the wrong subject and getting raked over the coals for it in the press. We've all seen it, and none of us wants to be that guy.

So how do we reduce the risk around real-time marketing? Here are two good starting points:

1) Data. Data helps get everyone on the same page. Using scorecards, metrics, projected impact, competitive performance, and so forth will turn your conversation filled with anecdotes and "we'll just see what happens" mind-set into quantitative research, performance goals, and projections. If you hadn't noticed, what I've been trying to do in this book is arm you with data to make the real-time marketing decision easier by showing that it drives performance improvements instead of just headlines. I've been trying to show the enormous growth of real-time marketing that is occurring not just with a few smaller brands but also with the most valuable brands in the world. Data can provide transparency, build trust, and set expectations that can not only guide your team but most importantly, reduce risk.

2) A Solid, Data-Driven Process. One of the biggest ways to reduce the risk is to have a strong process in place. With the right infrastructure, people, process, technology, and analysis in place, real-time social messages can appear to be shot from the hip, when they've actually been through a planned, cross-functional process that makes sure the brand is reducing the potential pitfalls throughout the event or everyday trend. A good plan and process are your best argument to gain executive support when they tell you that it's too risky, or that there are too many things that can go wrong. It's your life raft and your best friend. It will help you get the executive support, resources, and authority you need to get the most out of real-time marketing.

SHOWING THE REWARD

The other side of this equation is showing your executive leadership that there's real reward in real-time marketing. Hopefully, the first few chapters of this book drilled into your head the amazing performance that many brands are realizing from real-time social marketing. We'll want to use performance metrics to evangelize the benefits of RTM.

1) Show the success that other brands have had. Yes, we've reviewed overall industry averages and showed a lot of different ways to slice the data in this book, and you should absolutely use them to project ranges for what performance your brand can expect from in-the-moment efforts. Anecdotal examples, as long as they support the larger trend of RTM performance, can also be very powerful. Picking a brand that supports your overall story line (Is your brand not known for social? Show one of those. Is your vertical not one that necessarily fits with the traditional "social brand" label? Show one of those). can be a powerful way to get your point across and make the concept more real.

2) Show the adoption rate of your competition. In some corporate cultures, nothing gets people's attention faster than watching the competition do well. If that's what gets your executive team motivated, then use it to your advantage. Odds are there's at least one brand in your industry that you can use as an example of real-time success. Pull their RTM performance numbers, show anecdotal examples, and show that it makes sense for your vertical. There's plenty of room in real-time marketing for many brands from the same vertical. Once a successful brand has planted their flag, you can easily plant your own alongside it.

3) Build your plan, share your plan. Don't put your plans together and file them away in a subfolder somewhere where no one can find them. Be proud of them. Post them on the wall, on obnoxiously large poster board, and include estimates for the performance of RTM social content over normal social content. Send them to your executive sponsor, get them on board with the effort, and socialize the numbers internally. Share your plan and your planned success.

So, yes, building out a convincing plan to justify RTM is going to take some work. If you have nonbelievers at the executive level, or at any level, you'll need to put a plan together that demonstrates how to reduce risk and show the reward of your efforts. But, the truth is, anyone who is planning on building out a real-time marketing program should walk through these steps anyway, even if there isn't resistance from within the organization. You're going to build out a better program, achieve better results, and bring less risk to your organization if you take the steps outlined as we build out a data-driven methodology. Don't make someone else force you to do your due diligence and planning. Take the lead yourself. Planning through all scenarios and making sure you have the right resources, processes, technology, and data at every step of your RTM process is going to take you from randomly tweeting a few funny blurbs on a Sunday night to having a team with goals, a library of social assets, rapid analysis procedures, and competitive intelligence. Yeah, that sounds like more fun to me.

REGULATORS, MOUNT UP

Now that we're ready to convince the organization that real-time marketing can add value without too much risk, it's time to get started building. We're going to start our methodology not by building out the actual plan itself...at least at first. First, we need to create an infrastructure to insure success—to bring together the best pieces from every discipline and set the stage for world domination. That's right. We're going to start by building out our team.

The process of designing and staffing your RTM team is one of the most important ones to perform correctly, and won't be a one-time exercise in the realities of today's world. Team building has become an ongoing process as people drift more frequently between projects, teams, and even companies. Having a group ready for large tent-pole events will happen multiple times per year, and the ability to quickly assemble a quality team each time can give you a big advantage. Because many brands are also interested in using real-time on a daily basis, it becomes more and more important to understand roles and responsibilities for RTM year-round.

So let's break out the different roles and traits of each that will help build out a great real-time marketing team.

PROGRAM LEAD

That first word in the job title is very important: program. When you're building out real-time marketing capabilities for your company, you shouldn't just be planning a few projects that have no resemblance to each other. You're not doing short sprints that redesign the wheel each time, you're setting up a program—something that can be repeated over and over again, with the same processes, goals and KPIs, and execution. You want a process that learns from each prior engagement instead of having the past successes and failures sitting in a PPT document in someone's archive folder. It's ideal to have the Program Lead be a common thread in every real-time marketing effort the brand is engaging in over time. They aren't just leading the project, they are owning RTM within your organization.

Traits: Solid history of bringing teams together and leading the process for rapid discovery, planning, execution, and analysis. Can effectively lead teams of individuals who don't report to him/her. Has a lifeline to the executive sponsor, and enough trust and authority from the organization to execute without permission and micromanagement.

Communicates across silos and levels of seniority with ease. We're looking for a leader who can push a cross-functional group to successfully deliver results, and can learn from what's worked and not worked in the past.

Responsibilities: Forming and communicating responsibilities to the team. Setting goals and communicating status, results, and learning to the organization. If there's a war room for a big event, he or she is point on everything from scheduling the team to making sure there's pizza there on Sunday. Building out assets, processes, and technology to give the team the best chance to succeed at real-time marketing.

CREATIVE LEAD

The Creative Lead defines the vision for all social posts and media content around your RTM efforts. They know the brand inside and out and not only the technical side of the creative—voice, tone, style guide, brand guidelines—but also the goals for the quarter, any other campaigns going on, and the main value proposition the brand is looking to drive home. If your brand or agency is large enough to have multiple creatives on the RTM team, the Lead is organizing their workload, schedules, and responsibilities alongside the Program Lead.

Traits: Deep knowledge of the brand's creative efforts, those of the competition, and the brand's positioning. Ability to rapidly brainstorm and build out multiple responses to real-time events within a minute's time. Not set on all social efforts being perfectly polished, but understanding that posting a quick response is a crucial factor in RTM's being done right. Uses data as a critical input into creative process. Can excel in a brainstorming environment, where every good solution doesn't need to come from him or her.

Responsibilities: Leads research and preparation. Builds out scenarios and coordinates responses (from copy to media) with the team. In the war room, coordinates creative team around quick generation of creative assets.

COPY LEAD

Everybody in the room thinks they can write a great line or social response. Actually, everyone in your company probably thinks they can pull this off. But to be able to write copy that is true to the norms and restraints of the given social channel, that is smart and on-point, that adheres to the brand's voice and tone and is grammatically sound is a job for the professionals. Add to the list that all of that has to happen within a few minutes' time over and over again, and the list of people who can pull this off gets pretty small.

Traits: Ability to rapidly brainstorm and iterate on ideas. Ability to quickly copy edit and check creative for grammatical errors and typos. Deep knowledge and experience writing in the brand's voice and tone, especially on the social networks chosen for real-time marketing.

Responsibilities: Prepare brand responses across multiple social channels for anticipated scenarios. Quickly brainstorm responses in the war room with other team members for rapid response.

SOCIAL LEAD

Beyond creating the right creative and copy for RTM, the tactics and channels your team chooses to employ while executing a message can have a large impact on your performance. The Social Lead is the go-to member of the team for making sure you are using best practices while posting. That includes both the elements that go into the message (Should we include a hashtag, and if so should it be a widely used hashtag or one the brand can own? Should we pose a question to the audience? Include mentions of other brands or celebrities?) and the social channels the message should be posted to (Is this best for Twitter or Instagram?)

Traits: Knows not only best practices for general social network usage but also what works for the brand (our audience loves mentions of Bill Nye the Science Guy.) Has access to and experience with the brand's social media management platform to post messages. Knows social posting patterns of the competition and RTM brands in general to anticipate timing of response and other brands that might chime in on certain micro-trends. In other words: a data-driven social media juggernaut.

Responsibilities: Key member of the core brainstorming group for all preplanned and rapid response content. Prepares hashtag strategies and individual @replies strategies. Can prepare multiple variations of social media response across social networks and post rapidly.

ANALYST

I obviously think that Analysts are awesome. Analysts can show you things and help guide your strategy by giving you a view into actionable insights that you might not have thought about otherwise. Many people I talk to have a bad opinion of Analysts—they think of them as someone who takes weeks to ingest all inputs into their analysis and will only report back on Tuesdays, because we agreed on Tuesdays, so why on earth would you ask for it at the end of day on a Monday? Well, apparently those people have had bad luck and worked with terrible Analysts. That kind of personality is the last person you need on an RTM team. But the good news is that not all data people are like that—there's a new breed that loves doing quick-turn analysis and monitoring the competition to find a nugget of insight that can quickly be turned around for additional value. And that's the kind of Analyst you need on your team to fuel a data-driven approach to RTM.

Traits: Has deep knowledge within the social media space, and knows the brand's goals and associated KPIs inside and out. Can lead teams to define success and create a supporting measurement program. Can quickly digest large amounts of data and create insights on a micro-level, but also step back and see the 30,000-foot view during an RTM campaign. And obviously, good with math, statistics, number crunching, and digital measurement toolsets (social media monitoring, web analytics, etc.)

Responsibilities: A key part of goal definition, goal measurement, and dashboard design. Point on competitive analysis during an RTM campaign, monitoring the performance of a brand's RTM efforts, and communicating rapid analysis back to the team in real time. Does the same for overall trends and competitive RTM content to identify opportunities and avoid possible land mines.

LEGAL REPRESENTATION

Oh boy, who let this guy in the room? If you thought that the RTM team was going to get boring once you added an Analyst, then you're going to hate the Legal Lead. But, really, having a representative from Legal isn't going to hold you back—it's actually going to give you more opportunities. You're going to have the official ok, in real time, that what you're posting in an RTM environment is not going to get you fired. It's the social media equivalent of a "Get Out of Jail Free" card, and that's a good thing. Having a team member who can provide this guidance will reduce any approval cycles that can destroy the timeliness of any real-time effort, and make sure your messaging is not only relevant to your audience but also reduced in risk and child safe.

Traits: Brings full authority for a go/no-go on brand messaging and content questions, and fully understands the unique position an RTM team is in as far as required timeline for approvals. Understands the brand's regular social tone and voice, and can quickly brainstorm alternate suggestions when a message is deemed to be out of bounds. A sense of humor would also be nice.

Responsibilities: Sets up initial framework for what is permissible and what is out of bounds for a brand's social media messaging. Has availability during peak RTM times to quickly approve or offer guidance on quick-turnaround social media efforts.

Now, I'm already hearing what you're saying in your head: "That's great, Mr. Moneybags, but I don't have budget for that. If I had the dollars to put together a team like the one you're describing here, I wouldn't have needed to buy this book, because I'd already be a king of real-time marketing." Well, yes and no.

Part of the reason I'm detailing these roles is to give you ammunition to go and get that budget if you don't have it today. Instead of getting you and a guy named Gary in a room together for the Oscars and thinking, "We'll just figure this out as we go along, because Gary is a pretty funny guy on Twitter," you'll need a solid team in place to take full advantage of the opportunity in front of you. This breakdown is designed to help you design a team, but these roles can also overlap. The Creative Lead and the Copy Lead could be the same person if that person has the right background and skill set and you don't have the resources for a full build-out team. The Project Lead could serve as Lead Analyst as well, but I'd rather you make the case to get dedicated resources for each of these roles. They all have different experiences, their brains typically work in different ways, and the diversity will help you build a better product for your audience.

So, yes, this is an RTM Fantasy Team, but either way, these roles need to be represented in some manner in your cross-functional group.

ASSEMBLING THE TEAM

When it comes to large events where you want your brand involved in RTM, one of the challenges is realizing that you'll need to build a team that isn't fully dedicated to real-time efforts all year round. The Super Bowl, the Oscars, and the Grammys don't happen every day. Your team for these events won't be dedicated head count that will just sit around the rest of the year, waiting for the next big thing. These people have day jobs, and are already embedded somewhere in the organization. You'll need to find and recruit them for a temporary assignment, and then have them blend back into their daily lives as civilians. You'll need to do all this while still placing yourself in the best possible position for real-time success.

If you're planning to participate in everyday RTM, the following factors are important as well. You won't deal as much with the on/off nature of tent-pole events, but you'll still need to be careful in how you bring the team together. And, if feasible, you'd like for your daily team to include as many people from your big event teams as possible.

Here are a few things to look for as you're going through this process.

Recruit Those Who Love RTM: Do you have a Creative Director who brought up a recent RTM effort in the kitchen over coffee? Talk to him/her. Do you an Analyst who sends out an RTM summary after every big event, even if she isn't assigned to the war room? Talk to her. Bring in people who understand the power of real-time marketing and have already seen it work. Their learning curve will be less dramatic, and they'll come in with some great ideas out of the gate.

Recruit Those Who Have Seniority: The more senior people you can get on the team, odds say that you'll get stronger work. Plus, your RTM efforts will be more visible to the organization as a whole, and experienced team members who bring along a good degree of authority with them will attract other great people as well.

Don't Just Recruit the Youngest People You Can Find: I've seen the mistake where a brand or agency just hands all things social media over to their youngest employees, because "they must understand social better than I do." I probably don't have to tell you that this idea makes no sense. I'll always encourage diversity on any team, but don't forget talent and skill sets. Don't put people on the RTM team just because they are young, but if they happen to be young, then great for them.

Find People Who Work Well with Data, Even If It's Not Their Job: There's going to be a lot of data flying around at high speeds, so find people who are used to working with data and know when to embrace it and when to ignore it. Find people who believe that data is a critical piece of putting together a good strategy, but not people who will never go against what the numbers say. We use analytics as a tool to measure and predict, but creativity shouldn't always be dictated by past performance.

BEWARE THE PROCESS TRAP

Alright, now we've got our approval to do real-time marketing. We've got a crack team in place. We're all set to go. Well, almost. We should probably build out a plan, right? Of course, we should. But that will involve creating a process, which is both an art and a science.

Processes can be wonderful, helpful, amazing things. They can give team members guidance on the best next steps, lead teams to success with a goals-driven approach, and offer known, repeatable steps to do it all over again the next time. Strong processes got a man on the moon and got *House of Cards* approved for a third season. Processes can be good things.

Processes can also be arduous, terrible scapegoats that drag organizations into a sea of gray cubicle walls that create flocks of button-pushing employees watching the clock for 5:00 p.m. to finally come. Processes can be the worst thing about someone's job. They smell terrible, and the dogs are always bothering with them. They can be soul crushing and humiliating. I've worked at plenty of companies where process drags down morale, performance, and creativity. You probably have, too. Everyone seems to know the process is not working, but it's the way that things have always been done, so let's keep going wasting our time and brains doing things that don't matter. Processes can be horrible things. But don't worry, we won't build our RTM process like that.

Let's build a process that gives us the good results but avoids the dogmatic stuff, and that can help us make the most of our real-time marketing opportunity. Let's build a process that's as modern and flexible as the social media channels we are looking to optimize. Let's build a process that your team members *love*.

So what does a good process look like? A lot like a bad process, but with a few key differences.

1) A GOOD PROCESS SETS GUARDRAILS, NOT MANDATES

There's a big difference between providing some leeway with how things should work and telling people exactly how to talk, walk, and when to wake up in the morning. We'll build a process that offers guidance on how to best take advantage of the RTM environment, but won't break if a few things change. Processes should change as you learn—your team is different from another brand in another vertical, so things won't be exactly the same for both of you. Sorry to tell you, but your team will be different next year than it is this year—different personalities, roles, experience, and ideas. A good process morphs around people to get the most out of their talents. Bad processes work the other way around.

2) A GOOD PROCESS OFFERS A FAMILIAR ENVIRONMENT

The advantage a process gives us is that it's repeatable. It's known by the group—they don't have to relearn how to work together each time you start, execute, and wrap up a project. It's like going home at the end of the day—you know where to put your keys, you (hopefully) know the people in your house, and you know exactly where the bourbon is. Setting up a known environment—with timelines, roles, and responsibilities—is a freeing exercise. It gives team members a sense of comfort in not having to worry about those details and being able to concentrate on the other work they are so good at. Real-time marketing can be a chaotic environment if you let it be one, but process can help make it feel much more controlled.

3) A GOOD PROCESS IS FLEXIBLE

This is the one that most companies miss out on. A good process can be changed by the team at any time if something isn't working or something could be better. The focus should be on the end goal—in the case of RTM, getting increased engagement from the audience—and not on how you get there. One caveat here—you need to make sure there isn't one person on the team who thinks he or she gets to dictate how the process flexes. This is a team decision. If you have a team member who just does whatever he or she wants, kick that person off your RTM team. Yes, just like that.

LET'S BUILD A DATA-DRIVEN RTM PROCESS

So what are the key steps to creating a real-time marketing process in your organization? And even more importantly, to creating a data-driven RTM process, one that learns and uses data to optimize the channel and opportunity? Let's take a look.

Chapter 6

AIMING FOR REAL-TIME SUCCESS

PICTURE THIS SCENARIO: YOU'VE JUST COMPLETED your first big real-time marketing event. You've gone out and done the hard work of securing budget for real-time marketing efforts. You've set up a team, monitored trends during the show, and posted some amazing content, stuff that you can really be proud of. The next day you wake up in a "I Just Worked All Day Sunday" hangover and roll into work. As you take your first sip of expensive coffee, you sit down to write a summary of your RTM efforts to the executive team. But as the cursor blinks at the top of the blank page, you suddenly realize that you don't know where to start. How do you translate the impact of your work into something that will resonate across the organization? And more importantly, how do you know whether you really succeeded? Good questions.

As it turns out, you forgot to set goals. You forgot to set up targets for what your RTM efforts should achieve, and how to measure the results. You forgot the first step, one of the most important steps. You had an idea of what success should look like, but everything was moving so fast, there was no time to sit down and write everything down.

Well, if you've been working in digital for a while, you've probably heard the same types of excuses as I have in the past. We don't have time to set goals. We'll measure this the same way we measure everything else. No one around here sets goals for each campaign, and we never have. We've been around the block a few times, so we know what it's going to look like when we knock one out of the park.

Have you heard any of these excuses before?

Measurement may not be the most exciting thing on the planet, but you know what is exciting? Beating the competition. Making a huge splash in the industry. Exceeding your goals so you don't just look good, but your boss looks good as well. And you're not going to get to any of those places without goal setting and measurement.

A GOAL-DRIVEN APPROACH

We're going to talk about measurement in this chapter, but first I'm going to take you back to a more innocent time. A time before social media—when mobile phones were as big as suitcases, and before anyone knew that gluten was a thing. We're going to go on a journey back to my college experience in the late '90s. Ancient history, sure, but trust me, there's a point here.

You see, back in college, T-shirts were a surprisingly important element of our wardrobe. Where I went to school, hardly anyone really got dressed up for class (and based on some of the guest lectures I've done recently for undergrads, not all that much has changed). You'd just roll out of bed, rub your eyes, throw on a T-shirt and whatever, and get moving to class before the top of the hour. It was, now that I think about it, not that much different than working at an Austin start-up.

The reason I bring this up is that because regular old T-shirts were the main fashion accessory for me and my friends, the task of finding interesting, clever, and awesome T-shirts occupied way too much of our working memory, time, and attention. We created T-shirts for every party we threw, T-shirts that proudly proclaimed our allegiance to our freshman hall, and T-shirts for every cause or club or intramural sport you could think of. But one T-shirt that I saw all across campus stuck with me over the years. It was generally on the back of a tie-dye, short-sleeved shirt and proudly read:

"I'm not lost if I don't care where I'm going."

It was a simple, slacker-y saying that was both kind of profound and kind of antiestablishment, which was the perfect encapsulation of being a college sophomore in the '90s. It was kind of grunge, kind of "I went to a Grateful Dead show but just hung out in the parking lot," and a bit like something Ethan Hawke might say.

The reason this saying has stuck with me over the years is because it continues to pop into my head time and time again, but for a different reason than in college. Today, I think of the phrase as I talk digital and social strategy with huge, sophisticated brands all over the world. These are companies that manage multibillion-dollar advertising budgets alongside huge digital and social efforts. Many marketers still don't have goal setting and measurement baked into every campaign that they do. Marketers aren't wearing that T-shirt to work, but they might as well be. I can't get away from it, no matter how hard I try. It's not that marketers are lazy—it's just that many have never worked within a goals-driven environment and have never experienced the benefits of doing so firsthand.

I'm reminded of it every time I see an email about a brand running a campaign without setting goals first, which is to say: *every day*. I'm reminded of it every time someone asks how we should measure social media *after* a campaign has already been completed. It's like I'm back in my dorm room, playing three-man and trying to figure out corporate finance all over again.

Well, the industry is getting smarter, and if you're looking to stay ahead of your competition in real-time marketing, you'll need a goals-driven approach to get there. It used to be that social media was primarily used as an experimental platform. You fought for a slice of budget, without much data to back up your arguments, to try out tactics to engage your audience and see what the response would be. You didn't even necessarily need a target you were shooting for. You just wanted to try a few different messages, a few different approaches and see what would happen. Well, thankfully, social media has grown more sophisticated than that in recent years, and as any maturing platform...matures...teams also grow in how they measure success. But just using any old metrics to measure success isn't enough. Good social teams need to know what they are shooting for. Painting a picture of success allows you to share what you expect to achieve and helps guide every decision the team makes on the way. Without goals around your social efforts, you're still just feeling lucky for any engagement or sharing or brand mentions you receive out there. But you're not just lucky—you're part of a business, and you have enough data already at your fingertips to set a solid, realistic goal for your team to achieve.

Unfortunately, most people skip the goal-setting step altogether. They jump right to increasing page views or clicks, and never ask why. That's bush—bush league. Why? Because once you get a metric in your head, you fall in love with that metric. You report on a metric because it's easy to measure, and it's right there in your social analytics tools dashboard. What could be easier? But you never ask yourself why you care about that metric, or even what that metric represents. You're not sure why you're using that metric to gauge success, just that it's an industry-standard one that you're boss didn't push back on.

So let's do our best to fix that problem.

Any good data-driven approach starts with goal setting. It will serve as the compass to help direct our RTM efforts and make crucial decisions. Goals can not only help guide what content to create and how to measure success, they can also show us how to build the right team and secure budget for our efforts. Social is no longer a fad, and now more than ever you need to demonstrate that there's true, predictable value in the processes around social media (and now real-time marketing) that you've put in place.

Goals will make you legit. With goals in place, you'll no longer fear data. You'll *crave* it. Goals will get you more budget and will align your team on how to best execute. Goals force you to learn what works and what doesn't, and how to set better goals next time around. And goals don't just stand on their own. They require corresponding metrics. A retweet isn't a goal but a metric on how to measure the goal of getting your audience to share your content. A brand mention on Facebook isn't a goal but an indicator that your audience is talking about your new product in a social channel. Goals set the framework, and metrics measure the performance. But I'm getting ahead of myself.

SETTING YOUR SIGHTS

So what's the value of a Facebook Like? If you get four favorites on a Tweet, what's that worth? How about a retweet—that's certainly worth more, right? If I get a Like on Instagram, is it worth more than a mention on Twitter?

I get it. It's confusing. And not helping the cause are the one hundred people out there telling you two hundred different things on how to measure social media success, that they've figured out the true path to ROI if you use their tool. Based on their math, a follower posting a certain type of picture at a certain time of day is worth $2.45 for your brand. It's guaranteed. Put it in your spreadsheet. It came out of our computer, so I promise it's right.

Stop it.

I'm sorry, but I'm not going to tell you the value of every individual follower. There are plenty of ways to get there, but that's not what we're here for. Honestly, a follower is worth different things to brands in different verticals. Followers from different demographic groups are worth different amounts, as are followers that are on a social channel ten times a day versus one time a month. And most importantly, followers are worth different amounts based on what a company does with its social strategy, how they speak to their audience and monetize the channel. What we'll do here is not throw out any numbers around the value of a behavior, but instead concentrate on the big picture.

Social KPIs have always been a source of debate, and depending on who you ask, sometimes poorly defined. Terms like "engagement" and "social followers" appear instead of dollar signs. That's ok but it's not exactly hard science for those that come from a conversion-driven, e-commerce background. The good news is that despite what you may have read, there are good goals and measurements to track the success of real-time marketing efforts. Most people just miss them because they don't think through the process in the right way. We'll do that now.

ASK THE BIG QUESTION FIRST

Many people start a measurement conversation with a list of all the metrics they could possibly track. Others start with a tool, and see what the default metrics are on the main dashboard. This is why analytics get such a bad wrap. It's so much easier than that.

Let's just start with the easiest question in the world, and the hardest question in the world. Let's start with

What are you trying to achieve?

What are you trying to do with real-time marketing? Why even start? Do you want to increase the reach of your message? Right on. Do you want more engagement with your audience? Great. Do you want to create an e-commerce-focused social campaign? Perfect.

Many marketers have a problem with this question when they first hear it, and I completely understand why. The first few times you hear this, it can be intimidating. Out of the mouth of the wrong person, it can actually be downright offensive and insulting. But if used in the right way, it can help make the rest of your decisions so, so much easier.

Starting with the big question helps to frame the conversation and the entire campaign. It helps communicate to the team and the company what you're really trying to achieve. And while taking a step back and starting with a higher-level goal doesn't tell you exactly what to measure out of the gate, it will help other groups be able to help out with the effort as well. If the head of a social team tells me she's trying to get more followers on Twitter, it comes off as a tactical approach that her team is the best fit to execute on. If she tells me that she is looking to increase the size of her follower base so that campaign messages will have a larger reach, other teams (like email, direct-mail, events, etc.) could also have strategies to help impact this goal. Goals are a great starting point because your efforts are bigger than single metrics, and your team needs to know the root of why you're doing what you're doing.

Want to know the reason that people don't set goals as the first step? Because it's difficult. Because it's more boring than figuring out what the creative will look like. Because sometimes people don't meet your goals, and people hate getting in trouble when that happens. But it's the one step that successful businesses take that leaves their competition in the dust. Because even if you don't hit your goal with your campaign, at least you know you failed. And you can figure out what you should change for the next effort. Without goals, you can't even try to fix something that's broken—or celebrate when you crush your goal and leave your fiercest rivals in the dust.

So we'll ask ourselves that question, but first, let's think of one more thing that will make this process even easier.

YOUR GOAL PROBABLY ALREADY EXISTS

The problem people have with setting real-time marketing goals is that the first instinct is to come up with a whole new set of things to accomplish. I understand, because I've been there as well. But the truth is that your company already has a set of goals for the campaign, the quarter, the year. They are great goals and efforts that the company has already assigned very smart people and budgets to help solve. Wouldn't it be great if our real-time marketing efforts just worked to help support those existing goals?

Do you have "social" as a goal for your company? I hope not, but I wouldn't be surprised. Whenever a new channel pops up, it's normal to place it in its own silo. It's different. It's weird. It's experimental. It's easier to keep it in its own little area. But the downside is that social doesn't look like an integrated part of your business, and with this model, it probably isn't as integrated as it could be. You're not getting the most out of social because your brand isn't thinking about it in the right way.

How should real-time marketing work? RTM should support other goals that you have, such as driving more top-line revenue, increasing customer satisfaction, increasing customer retention. There will be a few new KPIs and maybe even a few unique goals with this approach, but overall, social is a layer on your current marketing and operational activities. And your real-time marketing efforts, and associated goals, should be no different. See? This is already easier than you thought it would be.

So now ask yourself the big question. Ask yourself what you're looking to achieve. If it's an existing goal (or multiple goals), then great. If not, then just make sure it makes sense with the overall push of the company. Got it? Good.

What type of goals can RTM impact? We'll dive into some more detailed examples in a few pages, but for now just know that most goals are set around the following buckets:

- increased engagement
- increased sharing of content
- building impressions
- generating revenue

Ok, let's keep going and talk more specifically about how to measure these goals.

HOW TO MEASURE

Now that we've got a big picture view of success, we'll need to go one level deeper. We'll need to know how we're going to measure and which metrics to use and eventually add to our dashboard. For this we'll use KPIs, which represent a handful of metrics to help us keep track of our progress.

The idea behind KPIs is that there are so many things you can measure that boiling your measurement strategy down to a few key ones will be essential for your sanity. Your goals will drive your KPIs for each campaign, project, or overall real-time marketing effort. By limiting yourself to a handful of KPIs, you'll keep your team focused on a specific definition of success and be able to track effectiveness without 50 different metrics on a giant spreadsheet that nobody reads.

Barry Cunningham heads up Fandezvous, a social media sports and entertainment agency. He believes that at this point in the maturity of RTM, clients are still looking for a lot of guidance from agencies and vendors for success metrics. He focuses on getting the audience to react, but also on what a client wants the audience to react to. Barry pushes clients to have a secondary action beyond hitting Like or retweeting. But this takes even more planning than just getting sample creative together. It means brands need to prepare by building out campaign elements like offers, sweepstakes, or some other form of secondary action that the brand wants to promote. To be effective, however, these calls-to-action need to be relevant to the conversation. "Secondary actions compel the audience to take action," Barry explains, "and activations are predicated upon giving people what they want."[1]

Social media is, and has always been, a mix of art and science. It's a conversation and not a billboard. Social media (and real-time marketing) doesn't work like traditional advertising, and the measurement strategy that brands use to gauge success needs to reflect that.

RAW COUNTS VERSUS RATIOS

The easiest, and most basic, way to measure social media is through raw counts of engagement. Counts of things like retweets and favorites are very easy to find and document. They are easy to compare to other social efforts. But they probably aren't the right thing for you to concentrate on. Let's walk through the following scenario to demonstrate why this might not be a good idea.

Situation: Doug leads up social media for his brand, which offers refreshing soft drinks at reasonable prices. Last year, Doug tweeted using the hashtag #SodaMarch during the month of March and received a good response. Now that it's March again, he is using the hashtag again and seeing an even bigger response. Doug happily puts together a report based on how awesome his campaign is performing year-over-year.

March, Last Year:
Average #SodaMarch Tweet Retweets: 125
Average #SodaMarch Tweet Favorites: 115

March, This Year:
Average #SodaMarch Tweet Retweets: 165
Average #SodaMarch Tweet Favorites: 152

Pretty sweet, right? Nice work, Doug. Except...there's another number that he left out of the equation that might let us know how well things are actually going for the #SodaMarch campaign: the number of followers his brand has.

Followers, Last Year: 110,198
#SodaMarch Retweets per Follower, Last Year: .11 percent

Followers, This Year: 245,432
#SodaMarch Retweets per Follower, This Year: .06 percent

Whoops. Now Doug's efforts don't really seem that good. His retweets went up by 32 percent, while his followers more than doubled. That's actually a decreasing engagement rate, but because Doug is looking at the raw numbers instead of a ratio, the true insight from the data is being hidden from him. He'll continue to do what he's doing, and while he's not necessarily doing any harm with his #SodaMarch campaign, he's missing an opportunity to understand that it's underperforming and how make it better.

What we need to look at instead is a ratio of actions per follower, for both retweets and favorites. If we know the percent of the follower base responding to our content, we can use that number to reset expectations as our follower base grows. After turning these metrics into ratios, we can see that this campaign might not be resonating with our audience and test new options for engaging followers. Remember, ratios beat raw numbers every time for actionable insights.

RTM MEASUREMENT AND REPORTING STRATEGIES

BUILD A DASHBOARD UP FRONT AND MAKE IT SIMPLE

During that first step (which is goal-setting, remember?), do yourself a favor and build your dashboard. You've probably either been building or digesting dashboards for years, but there's always been something a little wrong with them. Everyone is totally into them during the build phase, but then they go unchecked and unwatched for six months. It happens again and again and again.

So this time we're going to build our dashboards a little differently. A little smarter. Here's how:

Build the dashboard after you've set your goals and KPIs. Design it, and redesign it, on a whiteboard, in the room with your RTM team. Do it with the entire team. Don't let your analytics team run off and then surprise you with it later. Let the analyst lead the exercise, but have the team build it together. Why? For a few reasons.

Dashboards Should Be Simple

If you've just set the goals and associated KPIs for the RTM campaign, everyone in the room still has them as top of mind. They are hopefully excited about going out and building an effort to beat those goals. What better time to agree on a reporting strategy?

All KPIs Are Not All Equal

As you're setting goals, you should have primary goals/KPIs and secondary goals/KPIs. Laying out the dashboard with the team helps reinforce this idea. Primary goals should be represented as bigger pieces on the dashboard, and be higher up on the page. Secondary metrics can either support primary KPIs directly underneath them or be lower on the page. Either way, laying this out together will help emphasize what the team is shooting for.

The Dashboard Is More Than a Dashboard

It's more than just an Excel sheet that the analyst will fill out after the campaign is over. It's an artifact that should be posted and referred to throughout the planning and execution stages of the campaign. If you design your dashboard up front, people can refer back to it as they build toward the day of the RTM event. I've worked with many teams that kick off every meeting by reviewing the goals, and the dashboard (even if there's no data in there yet) is a great document to work through that target for the team.

SET UP A REPORTING CADENCE

Ok, we're almost there. We've got goals, based on reality, using ranges, and a solid dashboard. Now we need to set up our schedule for communicating results. What I recommend is that the dashboard is used only for Post-Event Reporting. Trying to fill out something in real-time as an event is happening is 1) not fun and 2) not useful. I think an Analyst can be doing about ten different things that are more valuable than that during the event. Let's talk through a few.

In-Event Analysis

During a big event, there will be craziness happening. The room will be filled with smoke (ok, not really, but it will feel like it), and your team will be keeping one eye on the event, one eye on your posts, and a third eye (?) on your competition. Who's talking about what? Did we miss something big that another brand already jumped on? And why does the competition keep posting on Tumblr? These questions will be flying around your head at ten thousand miles per hour. So, keep it simple.

1) High-Level KPIs for Your RTM Posts

Someone on the team should be keeping track of your posts. Set a time limit (5–10 minutes) to give your followers a chance to react to the new content you've posted, and then call it. Move on. But first, announce the number in the room, and be sure to mention whether it met the goal or missed the goal, and with a quick assessment, why.

2) High-Level KPIs for Other RTM Posts

Figure out who is getting the best response from the bunch.

3) Trends within Trends That Are Appearing

You'll need tools (whether sophisticated, homegrown, or simple) to identify new trends that are popping up and which brands that are jumping on them. Analysts are great at processing a large amount of data in their heads, so make sure they are heading up this capacity for the team.

Post-Event Analysis

Now's the time to use that dashboard. How did your stuff perform? How did other brands perform? Your best/worst? The overall best/ worst? What can you learn from the delta?

Post-Event Analysis is going to be one of the major keys to a data-based real-time marketing program within your organization. You need to be honest about how your team performed, critical about any flaws that emerged, and accepting of other RTM brands and wins they had. Learn from your own wins. Learn from the wins of others. Be honest in understanding that every brand will not have the same advantage for every event and micro-event. Arby's got a great response to the Pharrell hat partially because they are good at what they do, and partially because the hat is in their logo. McDonald's couldn't have done the same thing there, and that's ok.

1) Get Your High-Level Metrics Together by 10 a.m. the Next Day

After working all night on a big event, I know this one stings a bit. But, honestly, if your dashboard and KPIs are preset, getting your results together shouldn't be that hard. You want your high-level metrics and success story together on Monday morning for a very simple reason: the press may come calling. If they do, you want to put your best data-driven foot forward to have solid data around your success from the night before. But it's for PR, not for your team. That's for the next day.

2) Give the Team One Day Off from RTM, and Then Review the Dashboard

The event is over, so don't worry about meeting a few hours later to gauge performance. You'll need a day to gather your thoughts, and the extra day allows for one other piece of data that should be included in the post-RTM wrap-up, and that's a summary of press mentions.

3) Review Not Only Your Numbers But Press Summaries as Well

Comb Ad Age and Digiday. Get not only your performance numbers, but what people are talking about from the RTM event. Why are they talking about Brand X or Brand Y? Was it clever copy, fast creative skills, or just something that resonated with the brand voice? Which RTM brands are getting rave reviews?

4) Use the Post-Event Wrap-Up to Start Planning for Your Next Event, Now

Keep your dashboard top of mind—and within remote-control reach of your social team. As you start planning for your next RTM event, you'll want to base your goals on reality (remember that from earlier in this chapter?), and this event's RTM dashboard is your new reality. But why wait until the next event? Take ten minutes with the team and brainstorm new tactics for the next event while this one is still fresh in your mind. Tide used Vine videos and got a good response. Let's try that out next time. Pepsi reached out to Coke and called a truce—and followers loved it. Document your ideas, and then get back to your day job.

GOALS AREN'T HARD, BUT THEY AREN'T EASY EITHER

Once you get used to the process of aiming your sights on what you want your real-time marketing efforts to impact, you'll find more success and do better work. You'll understand not only what you're doing, but why you're doing it. It'll be more rewarding, and when people congratulate you for being so creative on the fly, you'll know that there's a lot more going on behind the scenes.

Chapter 7

THE DATA-DRIVEN
RTM PROCESS

WE'VE SEEN WHAT REAL-TIME MARKETING can achieve, how to construct a solid foundation for success, and how to make sure we're using a goals-driven approach. But now we're just sitting here with a bunch of resources and no idea how to build out our program in the right way. We want something that is flexible but repeatable. We want a process that team members understand and can rely on, but also one that doesn't crush the creative spirit that can make real-time marketing such an effective marketing tool. And, of course, we want to build a process that gives us an advantage by using data throughout to keep the team smart and goal driven. So, great, let's do all that.

Here's a five-step process that will help teams focus on a goals-driven approach (Figure 7.1).

Data will help us deliver some great real-time content to our audience, and we'll measure the performance of our efforts (and the efforts of others) at every step. We'll have data in our hands while making key marketing decisions, and understand the benefits and trade-offs of our actions.

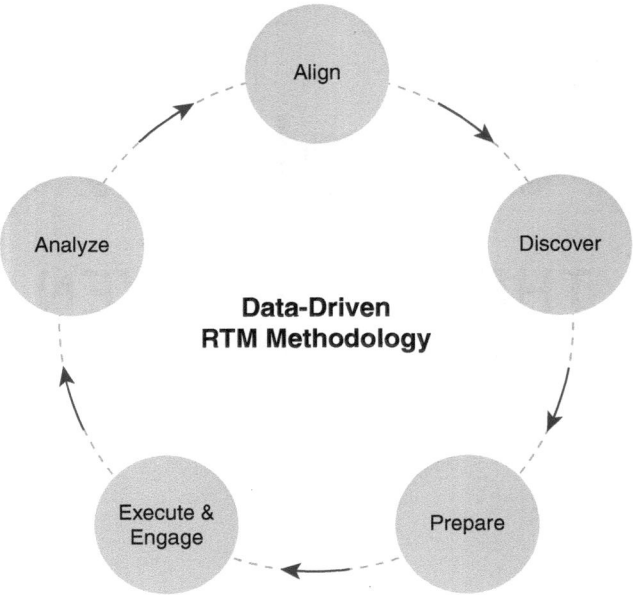

Figure 7.1   The Data-Driven, Real-Time Marketing Process

For each step, we'll look at the key components to making your RTM process successful through the following lenses:

- **People**: what are the key roles for each step, and who is taking lead on different efforts?
- **Process**: what are the steps and actions that will help build out a solid, repeatable program?
- **Technology**: what are the tools needed to be successful?
- **Data**: what pieces of data do we need at each step to prepare, execute, or analyze performance?

By the end of this chapter, you'll have an outline of how to build your own data-driven real-time marketing program that is flexible, gets the best out of each team member's skill set, and adds value each time your brand decides to engage in RTM. Sound impossible? Never tell me the odds.

One of the strengths of this process is that it brings data into real-time marketing if you're planning around either a big, tent-pole event or for an everyday real-time program. The main differences between the two approaches are timing and cadence:

- If your team is preparing for a tent-pole event, you will want to run through this process in the weeks leading up to the show to align and inform the team.
- For everyday real-time marketing, your team will want to run through this process on a regular basis, but not each day that your brand is tweeting. Monthly or quarterly is probably good enough, although more aggressive teams can do weekly check-ins.

Another point before we get started: if you read through all of the below points and starting thinking, "Man, this is a ton of work," please don't worry. What I've outlined below is a collection of best practices to infuse data into a brand's real-time process, but the intention isn't to make RTM feel like an overly burdensome practice. Brands can do RTM on a shoestring budget, by following good practices and processes (that, of course, include data) and without a huge team. The below thoughts are meant to cover all team sizes, from one-person operations to fully-stocked war rooms, so it's up to you what will work with your current organization and resources.

Ok, enough of the disclaimers. Let's see how data can help us perform better with real-time marketing.

DATA-DRIVEN RTM PROCESS STEP 1: ALIGN

As we reviewed in-depth, goal setting is the key to a successful campaign, project, or ongoing program. Goals are important because if they are being used correctly, they drive every other part of the process, soup to nuts. Starting your RTM process without goals might work out for you, but it probably won't be as good as it could have been.

We've talked about the best practices for creating a goal-driven real-time marketing strategy. Let's talk about how to kick off your process by using those tactics with your team and making sure your RTM effort is aiming in the right direction.

ALIGN: PEOPLE

- *Appoint a Leader to Own the Goals Process, but Keep the Whole Team Involved:* Everyone on the team should be involved in the goal-setting process, but someone needs to be point. The Program Lead, working alongside the Analyst, is a great choice. Why? He or she is the person in charge at the end of the day, and what better person to make sure the team is aimed at the right success than the person who will be held accountable for the results? Kicking off the goals definition process can also set the tone for the rest of the program or project, and establish the Program Lead as not just someone who schedules meetings but a strategic thinker leading an important effort.

- *Keep the Team Involved:* Another important consideration for your team is to make sure that everyone is involved in the goal definition. And yes, I mean *everyone*. To be clear, this doesn't mean that the Program Lead goes into a room, creates a vision of brilliance, and reports back to the team to present the goals for five minutes in a team meeting for a quick rubber stamp. You'll need at least an hour to sit down with the team and walk through the high-level goals as a group. Be inclusive when it comes to goal setting. People who are invested in the process will believe more in the resulting objectives, and you'll get a better campaign out of it.

- *Your Analyst Leads the Metrics Process:* Now that you've defined your goals, you'll also need to define how you measure those goals. This is the point where the Analyst takes charge—finding the best measurements that are accurate (and that include data sets that you'll actually have access to) to build out the plan for measuring. Doing this in a team setting is probably a mistake. Unless you have a team that has done this many times before, everyone will have their pet metrics that they've always used that might not be the best for real-time marketing. The Analyst can come back to the team to review which metrics will be used to track the high-level goals, and should always stay open to feed-back.

ALIGN: PROCESS

- *Set the Stage to Keep Goals Top of Mind:* Keep the goals of the project ever present by continually bringing them up in every discussion around choices being made, plan to post them publicly, and include them in any future success reporting for the rest of the organization.

- *First, Get Sign-Off From the Team:* Summarize your goals and recommended KPIs, and recirculate them back to the team before sending them off to the executive sponsor. Will this measure the success we are hoping for? Can we measure all of these things with the technology and people we have? Does this fit with our larger corporate goals? Are we all ready to sign up for this? If all of the above questions are answered with a "yes" from the team, then you're good to take it to the executive sponsor.

- *Now, Get Sign-Off from the Executive Sponsor:* Don't even think about emailing this over to your executive. When it comes to the conversation of goals and KPIs, you want it to be a conversation. Book a meeting. Walk him or her through the thought process that got you here, tell him or her that the team is on board and ready to start moving forward. Explain how this strategy is in line with the other goals you have on your plate as a social team, as a marketing organization. Get your executive team on board and you'll find that support, resources, and excitement about the event come with it.

ALIGN: TECHNOLOGY

- *Build Out Your High-Level Dashboard:* We've got goals. We've got key performance indicators. But where are they going to live? We'll need to build out a scorecard. Remember, dashboards are meant to tell us two primary things: 1) "How Did We Do?" and 2) "How Can We Do Better?" Dashboards should be designed to take quick action, action that is data driven and informed. As we discussed in chapter 6, involve your team in this process to make sure everyone is on board with how success will be tracked.

- *Design Your In-Campaign Reporting System:* During the event, you'll want a structure and mechanism to collect data about performance. Your team will need a way to quickly collect information about how your RTM content is working to make decisions, and understand whether the other RTM brands posting that day are hitting on trends that are resonating with the audience. Reporting will be happening at many checkpoints during the event, and new data will continue to roll in for each reporting period. This won't look like a dashboard, but there needs to be some system of communication defined within the team.

- *Create Artifacts to Help Communicate Goals:* Build out your dashboard, post metrics on the wall, or take over one of the big LCD screens in the office with your goals and metrics. Everyone should know that not only do you have an RTM program kicking off, but what company goals the program will be improving.

ALIGN: DATA

- *Set Goals Based on Reality:* The best way to set sensible goals is to look in the rearview mirror. Goals need to be set in the real world, and nothing is more realistic than similar events that occurred in the recent past. By understanding how our RTM worked and learning from the other efforts to say that we think we can do 10 percent, 15 percent better this time because we're learning how to do real-time more effectively, we can set a baseline each time for solid expectations. And don't forget to use ratios ("retweets per follower") versus raw action counts. This way you can end up with expectations based on your current follower count conditions.

- *New to RTM? Leverage the Competition's Performance Data:* Basing goals off your brand's past performance works for companies that have done real-time efforts before, but if you're just starting to get your feet wet with real-time marketing and still want to base your goals on some sort of sensibility, not to worry. There's a way to get there as well. To set goals for a new RTM program, you can go through the same process but use a competitor or other RTM brand's data to set a benchmark.

DATA-DRIVEN RTM PROCESS STEP 2: DISCOVER

As with anything in life, it's important to learn from our successes and our mistakes (but not necessarily in that order). If we're not acting like learning animals, we end up repeating the bad parts of history, and any success we see is simply due to luck. That doesn't sound like a lot of fun, so let's not do that.

The key to the Discover step of the Data-Driven RTM process is that you're gathering as much intel as possible to guide your real-time efforts. How many people will be watching the event coming up next week? How often do other brands chime in on random hashtags for everyday RTM, and what kind of return are they seeing? What can you learn about the event, the story lines that might come up, and anything else that can help give your content an advantage to be more relevant in the moment? That's the point of the Discover step.

If you're using this methodology to prepare for a large tent-pole or other big event, then the Discover phase will be a one-time occurrence (until next year's event.) For Watchlist or Everyday RTM, the Discover phase should happen on a regular cadence—once a month, once a quarter—to understand how the social world has changed since your team last performed this exercise, and to gather more data around new tactics that your team should be trying.

DISCOVER: PEOPLE

- *It's Everyone's Job to Learn:* You're looking to gain an advantage by learning everything you can across every discipline, so don't hand the learning off to just one person. The Discover step of the Data-Driven RTM process not only gathers great data to arm your team with high levels of intelligence but it helps immerse the team in the subject matter at hand. You want everyone's head in the game, and having everyone do research is the best way to kick off this journey.

- *Be Specific with Topics by Role:* Don't set the team off with a vague, "Go learn everything and anything you can," and then hope for the best. While you want everyone involved, you also want to provide direction to avoid duplication and blind spots. Assign any team members you might have to research specific subjects, and match topics with subject-matter expertise. Divide and conquer.

DISCOVER: PROCESS

The Discover process is pretty simple as long as the Program Lead is providing direction and communicating expectations. Here's a good example of an effective way to get the most from your team's Discover efforts:

1. *Set the Agenda:* Review the task at hand and give each team member an area to focus on. Walk through all of these areas with the greater team to get feedback on any missed opportunities that aren't covered in the current plan. Set expectations with the team on what your definition of "research" means—it's probably not just doing a few Google searches, but rather it's about coming back with tangible findings they can present and share with everyone. Set an agreed-upon time frame for research and make sure there are good communication channels set up between team members during this phase—group email accounts, common folders, and so forth.

2. *Let People Go:* It's up to the Program Lead to help do some lead blocking and clear the team's calendar during the Discover phase. Research won't be taken seriously if it's considered a "Can you do this for an hour tomorrow night?" exercise. Give people time to dig in, learn, and prepare materials to share with the team.

3. *Bring Them Back:* Book a few hours and have each team member present (yes, present) what they've learned. Encourage them to use examples and data to back up anecdotes.

4. *Review Recommendations*: Ask each team member to create a one-slide summary of what steps the team should take based on the research they collected. The team may come up with more recommendations and tactics to test based on the presentation, but start with a simple list of actionable insights.

You should end this step with great data and a list of recommendations, not all of which will make it through the next phase, but keep them documented as you move forward.

DISCOVER: TECHNOLOGY

The technology you'll want to leverage during the Learn phase will be fairly diverse depending on the subject matter being researched. The topics your team will be researching can be as creative as your tactics for RTM, but here are a few go-to categories of research tools to use.

- *Social Media Search Tools:* When heading into a tent-pole event, knowing what was discussed on social media the year before can be a huge benefit for any RTM brand. Understand which pieces of RTM resonated with the audience the most, and figure out posting patterns around timelines for the event. Did CPG brands post during the Golden Globes red carpet? Is the halftime show a time to be silent or chime in? Do brands get better performance in the first half or the second half of the event? Social media search tools that can go back at least one year can help build out a model of recent history, and allow you to take advantage of any patterns or opportunities you can find.
- *Trend Identification Tools:* Understanding what is trending in the days leading up to the big event can give your team a big advantage. If you know which story lines are active not only in the media but also on social networks, it gives your brand a leg up to understand what might resonate during the event as well. Trend identification tools allow you to look across multiple geographies to find trends, understand when brands are

chiming in on the conversation, identify the top content that is being discussed, and even predict the direction in which the trend will head based on historical patterns. Arm your team with an understanding of the event beforehand, and your planning will cover more ground.

DISCOVER: DATA

Data for the Discover phase, much like the technology your team is using to gather information, will be fairly diverse and reflective of the event or campaign you're focusing your research on. Make sure you cover all your bases with the data you are collecting for your team by concentrating on the following buckets:

- *Start With Your Own Data:* If this isn't your first pass at RTM, how did you do last year? What worked and didn't work? What were your takeaways after the last event about why you did so well (or why certain messages may have flopped)? Don't let past performance live in a drawer somewhere, even if it wasn't your best moment. Learn and grow.
- *Event Data:* For a big event, you'll want to find brands that did RTM the year before by searching past news reports that include a real-time marketing wrap-up for the event (Digiday and Mashable often do these.) But beyond social, what's all the other information you want to know about the event? You'll want to make sure you know the start time for the preshow and the event start. If the event has a host, who is it and what do they usually talk about on social media? What's the expected viewership (and last year's viewership numbers)? What are some known micro-events within the event (halftime show, nominees for different award categories, performers, etc.)
- *Story lines:* Going into every big event, the media identifies and amplifies story lines that they know will resonate with the audience. Maybe one of the quarterbacks in the Super Bowl is a hometown hero, or an independent film with a tiny budget

received four Oscar nominations this year. If you see these top-ics are being pushed by the press before the event, you should be ready when they make an appearance during the event. Story lines can also be tracked for Watchlist content, as well to understand any possible weekly or monthly topics that you want to monitor for breaking news.

- *Press:* Some brands even telegraph their intentions before a tent-pole event, leveraging their PR teams to get press talking about how sophisticated and forward-thinking their social media war room is, and they can sometimes tip their hand in identifying some RTM strategies ahead of time.

DATA-DRIVEN RTM PROCESS STEP 3: PREPARE

The Prepare phase is when all your hard work comes together. The out-put of this phase is your game plan to perform real-time marketing with confidence. Your team feels ready to act for a few scenarios that have a high probability of happening, and has a solid process in place to act on unforeseen events as they pop up.

Josh Martin, the Director of Digital & Social Media at Arby's Restaurant Group, Inc., believes that preparation is the true differentia-tor for brands to realize real-time marketing success.

"For us, preparation is key. We try to work as much in advance as we can and plan out these events so that we can build content for them. We know when the Super Bowl or Oscars or Grammys is coming, and we work a month or two in advance and get a calendar of big events that we want to create content around and participate in. We identify which events we want to align ourselves with." Martin estimates they only end up using maybe 10 to 20 percent of all the content they create around different scenarios for tent-pole events, but that the preparation pays off in establishing the ability to be agile and timely with the post-ing of content. "We think about different scenarios that could happen that can be planned for so we have content ready to go and we can pull the trigger very quickly. The biggest part of RTM is the timeliness of it—to repeat the wins we've seen out there, you need to hit the news feed very quickly and watch it amplify and grow before you miss that opportunity."[1]

PREPARE: PEOPLE

- *For a Big Event, Prepare the Team for a Full Day's Work:* Tentpole events are becoming more and more a full-day affair, so make sure you've got your team prepared and expectations are set. News and story lines will start rolling in the morning of the event, so you should have at least one team member monitoring social networks and news outlets for breaking updates that might change your game plan. If the event is scheduled on a weekend, the Program Lead should try to get the team that Friday off to spend with their families/friends and then be ready to roll. The team will need a place to work (either a war room setting with everyone on point, a distributed environment where people are working from home but still communicating, or a hybrid) and communications channels during the event.
- *Everyone Should Know Their Role:* This is the time to pressure test the roles on the team to make sure everyone understands expectations for the event. Who is monitoring the competition? Who is checking for new trends on social, and who is watching the event itself for story lines and points to jump into the conversation? Get this settled and agreed on before game day.
- *Team Members Should Have Resources Ready:* Each team member will have a different set-up during the event, but make sure that everyone has thought ahead and prepared accordingly. Prebuilt assets will need to be quickly found and brought in with new copy, numbers will need to be pulled, and social listening tools will need dictionaries of terms set up for tracking. Get all of these ready before the show.

PREPARE: PROCESS

Bring together the data you've researched, and from it, build a plan of attack for the event. As a team, you'll need to form your game plan and decide how to approach the event. Which story lines will resonate with the audience you're looking to attract? Which topics are out of bounds? And most importantly, which tactics will help you realize your goals for your RTM campaign?

- *Scenario Planning:* Spielberg wins the Oscar. There's a blocked field goal. A performer slips on the stage—how will you react (or will you just let it go)? From your research, you'll come up with a number of potential scenarios that may occur during the event. The more you can prepare around those scenarios, the less you'll be scrambling to create copy and creative to try and be the first to jump into the conversation after the fact. But with millions of different possibilities for what could happen during the event, how do you prioritize your scenarios? Two factors: probability and payoff, should guide this decision. Probability should be self-explanatory—if there's a high likelihood of something happening, then the priority for you to be ready for the event goes up. Payoff is the second factor—what is the potential return your brand could receive by being first to chime in on a certain subject? For example, if the host mentions that he or she is hungry for pizza during a major awards show, the payoff to have quick creative ready for DiGiorno, Pizza Hut, and Papa Johns would be much higher than Audi—so pizza brands would prioritize that scenario over others.
- *Establish Guidelines:* Knowing what is in bounds and out of bounds around language, topics, and creative can help save a lot of time and frustration during the RTM process. It makes sense to do this work ahead of time and have a go-to set of guardrails that the social team can rely on. Rod Strother, the Director for the Digital and Social Centre of Excellence at Lenovo, has built

out a framework to make sure his social team understands both the boundaries and optimal tactics for social media. "There are obviously brand guidelines around tone of voice and everything else, but we've also produced social guidelines for the team. We've created a social cookbook that outlines not only how team members can use individual social platforms, but how they can get the *best* out of each platform. It walks through our social strategy and outlines the rules of engagement." Lenovo provides enough detail to give social teams a solid understanding of the guidelines they want to follow, but without detailing specifics for each market where they operate, where social channels and norms can vary greatly.[2] The practice of empowering the social team with knowledge instead of requiring approval for every post gives the team a mix of freedom and structure that allows them to be more creative and, more importantly, post timely responses, a key part of staying relevant and viable in the RTM world.

- *Establish the Decision-Making Process:* As you plan, a crucial step is to detail and communicate the decision-making process to the team. In the heat of the war room, many ideas will be flying around for a diverse set of topics, and you need to make sure that while all team members should be submitting ideas for a relevant response from the brand, there needs to be a process for a go/no-go on each one. Establish who makes the final call on the direction of each post, and that you're bringing goals into the process each time by asking, "Will this drive us toward our goals?" during the brainstorming process.

PREPARE: TECHNOLOGY

The purpose of technology in the Prepare phase is to get your ducks in a row before jumping into real-time, and having all the resources your team will need ready to go. The last thing you want is to miss out on a potential in-the-moment opportunity by not having a platform or asset at your fingertips.

- *Prepare Your Assets:* Get your content ready. If your scenario planning resulted in some good prebuilt content, then make sure it's locked and loaded. Another good way to be ready to act is to build out templates—creative executions that include the framework of potential posts in a brand-friendly environment so that your creative team can add the right media and copy, and then quickly publish.

- *Prepare Your Social Platform:* Your social tools (both for posting and monitoring) will need specific settings for an RTM event, so make sure the technology is ready to go. Time is of the essence during a real-time event, and to be relevant to the audience you'll need your social platform queued up for instant publishing.

PREPARE: DATA

- *Make Sure Your Tactics Are Measurable:* As you are finalizing your plan, review your approach and make sure all of your tactics include measurable elements. Will you be including trackable links to third-party sites or microsites within your domain? Make sure any pages have been tagged with web analytics tracking and that the team has access to that data during the event.

- *Always Ask: How Will This Impact Our Goals:* Step back and look at the plan you've worked hard to create, and make sure that the team managed to stay on track with your end goals. A key to having a data-driven, real-time marketing plan is to have all the final tactics and execution support what you're trying to achieve. It's easy to get excited about a certain topic or strategy and forget the aim of the overall program, but a good team will keep itself in check and make sure they are designing marketing efforts that will result in success. If some of the tactics are off, now is the time to adjust and revise.

- *Make Sure the Team Understands How to Use Data During Execution:* Work with the team to agree on how to use data to build out an advantage for your brand. You can use data to quickly recognize new trends, find success that other brands are having with specific tactics and topics, and rapidly measure your own team's success to make the call on whether you'll continue using different aspects of your social strategy. Prepare the team to understand that data will be playing a part in the decision-making process so that there are no surprises when the quick decisions need to be made.

DATA-DRIVEN RTM PROCESS STEP 4: EXECUTE & ENGAGE

So, here you are—it's time to get to work. Whether you're kicking off an everyday RTM program or it's the day of a big tent-pole event, your team should be ready to execute a great real-time campaign. You've worked with the team to set goals, learn as much as possible, and formulate all that data into a solid plan.

Notice that this step isn't just called "Execute"—there's that tricky second piece to creating RTM content, "Engage", as well. Because real-time marketing is part of a conversation, it leaves open the opportunity for repeated messages as topics evolve and as the audience responds to a brand's initial post. Posting solid content isn't the end of the road here—you need to stay on top of topics and decide whether reengaging makes sense as well.

EXECUTE & ENGAGE: PEOPLE

- *All Eyes on Trends:* As new trends emerge, make sure the entire team is empowered to help identify good candidates for topics that can result in great in-the-moment content. You'll hopefully have a good technology system set up to identify Trending Topics, topics that other brands are chiming in on, and anything else you've decided can give you an advantage in finding great content. But even with a good technology backbone, don't be dogmatic about where trends come from. Good content from any potential source should be considered.
- *Foster a Creative Environment:* If you're creating a war room environment, make sure you have an area where people are assembled

to make for an easy flow of information and ideas. Gather the team members a few hours early so no one is feeling rushed or behind the curve. Remind everyone of the process before the event kicks off, but also agree when the process can bend. Remember, your RTM framework and data are here to help the team, not to hold it back, so make sure the team knows which parts are essential (like legal guidelines) and which are a "nice to have" (like using certain prebuilt templates). For Watchlist and Everyday RTM, make sure that lines of communication are set up in advance so you can act quickly and with quality content.

- *Ideas, Ideas Everywhere:* You've hopefully assembled a great team that has great insights from each of their respective areas, so make sure you're using them to their full potential. If you're the Program Lead, make sure you're creating an environment where people can easily chime in with ideas around your strategy and breaking trends to get all ideas out on the table. If you're in another role on the team and submitting ideas as trends unfold, make sure the ideas are in line with your strategy and support the goals that your team has created. Don't be shy about brainstorming, but also don't distract with a stream of ideas that aren't aimed at accomplishing what your team is there for.

EXECUTE & ENGAGE: PROCESS

The real-time marketing framework that your team has built out is designed to ultimately accomplish one thing: *to make good, fast decisions.* Make sure you're leveraging the assets, learning, and planning you've put in place to do exactly that. Sometimes, in the heat of the moment, it's natural to just throw everything aside and go back to relying on chaos—let's not do that. Work the process that you've built and deliver real-time content that is goal oriented and relevant to your audience.

- *Trend Identification:* As topics and trends emerge, float them to the team as potential content candidates. If you have a good tracking system in place, you should be able to track mentions and sentiment around the subject to help inform your decision-making process.

- *Triage:* Once you have one (or multiple) candidate(s) for a trend to jump in on, triage the idea with the cross-functional team. Make sure the topic is on-brand and within legal boundaries, and then start a quick brainstorming session around your brand's take on the topic. Include all aspects—copy, creative, and an understanding of how other brands are jumping on board. If you have premade creative around the subject, would it be good to post as-is or does it require tweaks? Make quick decisions, always asking in the back of your head, "Will this help us to accomplish our goals?" As we discussed in the Prepare step, you've already nailed down a decision-making process for the team. In whatever way that's happening—whether it's the Program Lead making the go/no-go call or a different process—make that call now.

- *Post and Monitor:* Once you've posted content, keep an eye on both your content and other RTM content around the same subject. How is your post performing versus other posts (and the performance goals you've set beforehand), and how are other brands doing on the subject? If there is a consistent high-performing trend, there may be the opportunity for a follow-up post on the same micro-trend.

EXECUTE & ENGAGE: TECHNOLOGY

Your technology solutions, no matter how basic or advanced they might be, should already be set up and ready to roll by the time you begin executing on your RTM campaign. Keep the following thoughts in mind as your team executes:

- *Watch All Screens:* When it comes to everyday RTM and big events, no screen rules over any other. Finding something interesting on a television broadcast can bring a brand as much relevance as a Trending Topic on Twitter. Broadcast events may take a few minutes to show as an official trend, so keeping many sets of eyes on the television will keep your team up to date. On the other side, some trends that pop up on social networks during events have little to do with the broadcast (like some Brand-to-Brand RTM and any preplanned content from other brands.) Make sure the team is staying on top of micro-events from every angle.

- *Keep an Eye on Other RTM Brands:* It used to be that by chiming in on a trend, you might be the only brand in the conversation—but times have changed. During a big event, a number of brands will be working to gain a share of attention from the audience. Make sure you're identifying the brands receiving the largest response from their followers, as well as watching a shortlist of your competition, to stay on top of the current state of RTM. If you see a strategy working well for another brand, bring the team together to discuss whether the same might work for your brand to accomplish your goals. Don't be a copycat, but stay nimble. The same can be said for Watchlist and Everyday RTM—pay attention to what other brands are doing well, and make a decision about whether it would be a good strategy for your brand to test.

- *Watch Audience Reaction and Sentiment:* In addition to monitoring what other brands are talking about, keep watch of how the audience is responding. If you monitor brand mentions during a trend, you can often get a good gauge on how the audience feels about real-time efforts beyond just looking at retweets and favorites. Social sentiment and language reacting to recent trends can help guide your decision-making process as well.

EXECUTE & ENGAGE: DATA

While working data into your RTM process, you'll need to remember that the numbers we've been looking at in this book have all been retroactive—that is to say, the results have mostly been decided. As a trend or big event is happening, numbers will be flying around like crazy—new data points, success metrics needing to be repulled and reanalyzed, and new topics to understand. Technology, a good process, and a solid Analyst can help turn this craziness into an advantage.

- *Quickly Move from Data to Insights:* Trends come and go quickly, so making a quick call on the viability of a topic is key during the Execute & Engage phase. If an Analyst has a good system together (a collection of process, technology, and data) going into the real-time event, he or she should be able to pull together metrics quickly and accurately. But metrics aren't the only thing that a Data-Driven RTM Methodology is built to create—we're looking to make good, fast decisions with the data. Make sure the Analyst is confident enough in the numbers and the RTM space not only to get the data in a fast fashion but to also make his or her recommendation for a go/no-go on the trend.

- *Catalog Unused Ideas:* As ideas pop up, some will not fly for one reason or another. Maybe a few other brands already jumped in on a subject, and your team doesn't think you want to be the fourth voice on a Trending Topic. Maybe your team wanted to post a piece of premade creative during the halftime show, and thought it was better than the micro-trend that just popped up. No matter what the reasoning, a brainstorming environment always creates a long list of unused ideas that generally disappear, never to be seen again. But there are great potential learnings—and great data—in these unused ideas, so don't allow your team to fall into the same trap. As ideas pop up, make sure someone is cataloging the ideas you used and didn't use (and why you didn't use them) so as to make your team smarter in future campaigns. You're not only collecting data every time you participate in RTM but also creating data.

- *Leverage Data, But Don't Let it Handcuff You:* As your team works through the process, you've put yourself in the best place possible by including data in every step of the preparation and execution—but don't let it become your worst enemy. Smart teams understand that data can empower a group to act quickly and act wisely, but if you rely only on data, or hold back on your decision-making process until you get more data, your RTM efforts can easily fall flat. Keep your eyes on the big picture—a goal-driven approach, and data to support your ideas and concepts—but don't let data slow your team down.

DATA-DRIVEN RTM PROCESS STEP 5: ANALYZE

The process has taken us through an RTM event, or a series of everyday trends, and we've now arrived at the stage where we look back on our performance. Even in an RTM program that is constantly on, smart teams set checkpoints to understand how their content is resonating with the audience, if goals and objectives need to be updated, and where new opportunities may exist. The key to this process is collecting data for the RTM campaign and comparing it to your goals. Or, said another way, how did we do, and what can we do better?

ANALYZE: PEOPLE

- *Gather Analysis Ideas from the Entire Team:* You'll have a core report for success that your Analyst will be in charge of creating that includes performance against your goals, and any take-aways and insights that come from the data. But the analysis of RTM shouldn't stop there—it should also include other topics and insights based on different directions the real-time conversation went during the event or campaign. Maybe a competitor knocked it out of the park—now is a great opportunity to do a quick deep dive on why they did so well, or more specifically, which tactics they used that your team can learn from. Maybe a Brand-to-Brand RTM effort between two other brands seemed like a good idea, but the team isn't sure about its performance. Gathering questions from the entire team about events that happened during the RTM campaign, and then prioritizing the questions so as not to overload your Analyst, will help give your team a wider view of insights from the event.

- *Takeaways for Everyone:* When the final core RTM report is presented to the team, make sure there are takeaways across all disciplines that are included. Did certain pieces of creative seem to resonate? Certain words, phrases, or punctuation? The use of hashtags on one social channel but not another? All of these learnings will help you not only create a better overall RTM strategy for the next campaign, but they will also help each team member get better at their individual roles.

ANALYZE: PROCESS

- *The Analyst Leads Reporting:* This should come as no surprise, but the Analyst on the team will lead the data gathering and analysis process. If he or she has set up the measurement strategy and technology infrastructure to get the right metrics, the data-gathering piece of this exercise should be pretty fast. The Analyst should also take a first pass at finding insights from the data, but as you'll see next, he or she isn't the only one.

- *The Team Creates Insights:* The Analyst should bring the team together after the RTM campaign to show the final results, and share the Analyst's initial findings from the data. This is when the process becomes a team effort. Now team members should chime in with insights from their point of view, and introduce any additional questions for the Analyst to investigate. The result here should be a document that includes not only hard data around the performance of the effort but also a list of five to ten best practices from the event, and five to ten steps to take differently the next time around. Including these insights on the final success report will help elevate the discussion around the success of the event as the report gets circulated beyond the core team.

- *Circulate to Wider Team:* No report should ever be created and then just filed away—reports are meant to share information about how a project performed and what the team learned. Get the report out to a wider team after it's been through enough cycles with the RTM team to be ready for prime time. Don't send it out before it's ready, or before you've discussed ideas around insights from all members of the team—you want to make sure the entire team stands behind the numbers and outcome from the campaign.

ANALYZE: TECHNOLOGY

- *Utilize the Infrastructure You've Built:* All data in the core report should be available from the core toolset you've built out, but any other ad hoc analysis may require more digging. It's hard to predict which questions will arise from the data, so just make sure you have a good number of resources that allow you to access different types of data (social listening, competitive performance, etc.) as needed.

- *Book a Meeting to Review:* Never just send a report via email. Booking a meeting underscores the importance of the campaign, and allows your team to walk others through the goal-driven process and results you saw. Meetings let you tell the story of the data instead of just sending out numbers, and that benefits all sides.

- *Follow Up with a Portable Report:* When it comes to finally generating a report to share throughout the company, don't rely on a proprietary technology and expect others to come to you. My basic rule of thumb is that if a report requires a login, your audience automatically gets cut in half. Take the extra step and export a report to Excel or PDF, or create the report in Excel in the first place, and distribute the document in any form that you think it will get noticed (email attachment, embedded image in an email, hard copy on your boss's desk, etc.) If you're sending it via email, include the key takeaways in the email text. Don't think that just because you created a report that others will do the hard work of seeking it out and finding it—you need to market your success.

ANALYZE: DATA

Your post-campaign report should include your core success metrics, plus any additional analysis your team asked for. Here are a few best practices around generating these reports.

- *Group Metrics by Goals:* You went to all the hard work of establishing and agreeing on goals. Now's not the time to hide those away. Be sure to put them front and center, and have the supporting metrics for each goal in the same section. If you're using three metrics to show engagement, lump those together in the "Engagement" section. Sounds simple, but you'd be surprised how many people ignore this step and just throw metrics all over the place. Design matters.

- *Include a Section for Takeaways:* Remember our primary two reasons for creating a reporting structure in the first place—showing how we did, and showing how we can do better. You don't want your takeaways to live in a PowerPoint file. Well, they can live there, but they need to be cohabitating in your scorecard as well. Why? Well, scorecards should be designed to be shared. They should fit onto one page that can easily be posted on a wall, attached to an email, or used as a desktop wallpaper (kidding) for anyone across the company. If you include your insights from the event in your scorecard, those details travel along with the data. Plus, when you're kicking off your next event, you want to quickly find the best practices from last time. No better place to hide those learnings than in PowerPoint or email, where great ideas go to die. Include them in your scorecard—it will tell the story of the data instead of just being a bunch of numbers. Remember: smart brands make their own data.

- *Get It Out Fast:* If real-time marketing has taught you anything, it's that jumping on trends can help brands grab some attention with less energy. Why wait a week when everyone's mind is on the next big thing? I don't think you need to create the report the night of the event. That's pushing it. The team is already probably working on a weekend or an evening, so why make it worse? Get your results and insights out to internal influencers while the iron is still hot, but not fast enough to crush your team's spirit.

AND THAT'S IT

See, that wasn't so hard. Creating a Data-Driven RTM process is really just a good amount of common sense, making sure the team is all pointed in the same direction, making timely and informed decisions in the heat of the moment, and learning what works and what doesn't. Using a process like the one above will help bring some method to the real-time marketing madness, and should give you an advantage over other brands that are truly flying by the seat of their social media pants.

Now that we've created a solid framework for doing RTM in the present day, let's take a look at where the real-time trend is headed in the future, and what opportunities exist for brands that aren't afraid to take a few risks.

This page intentionally left blank

Chapter 8

THE FUTURE OF RTM

WE'VE BEEN ON QUITE A JOURNEY so far—looking at how brands use Twitter, bringing data to real-time marketing to show what works (and what doesn't work), and understanding how brands and media companies can leverage in-the-moment trends to improve engagement with their audience. And now that we've built out a framework for bringing data into every part of a brand's RTM strategy, how do we plan for the future? And what does the future of real-time marketing even look like?

As RTM has evolved over the past few years, we've already seen a good number of shifts in strategies and tactics. Brands have jumped in to experiment with one or two real-time posts during a large event, or jumped on a random Trending Topic to see if the audience would follow along. We've seen brands chatting with each other to try and draw the audience in, brands creating their own sideshows to major award shows via custom hashtags, and even brands typing out nonsensical Tweets with plenty of misspellings to draw attention (I'm looking at you, J. C. Penney). Some tactics have worked and some have fallen flat, but the wide array of different methods being used with RTM shows that brands aren't afraid to experiment with the practice. With new brands jumping into real-time every day and all the new functionality coming to social networks each month, the rates of experimentation shouldn't slow down anytime soon. When any ecosystem sees rapid growth, what is considered "the normal way of doing business" is due to change rapidly. Not all new tactics show performance bumps, but you can be sure that the ones that do will be rapidly adopted by brands and media companies to capture the audience's attention.

So let's take out the crystal ball and, knowing what we know, see what changes and disruptions real-time marketing should experience in the next few years. How will brands continue to stay relevant as technology improves, social media teams become more experienced, RTM processes become refined, and data becomes more robust?

REAL-TIME EVOLVES

In a hypergrowth area, predicting more growth is an easy thing to do. As we saw in chapter 1, brands are flocking to real-time marketing but there's still more room for growth. Less than a third of the Interbrand 100 participated in RTM during the 2014 Super Bowl, and that number should grow in future years. But as time continues and technology advances, RTM might look a bit different when new brands finally hop on board. Here are a few ways real-time should evolve in the next few years.

THE AUDIENCE WILL CONTINUE TO BECOME MORE REAL-TIME FOCUSED

Marketers follow their audience, and our world is becoming more real-time every day. New social networks, new devices, and new levels of integration between real-time media and the technologies that promote audience participation are growing each year. The audience's expectation for real-time, all of the time, will only continue to grow.

As the audience becomes more trendcentric, advertisers should follow suit. In a few years, it may be the case that advertisers who don't have a view of current topics that are top of mind for their consumers will be at an extreme disadvantage in attracting and holding their attention.

REAL-TIME MARKETING WILL BECOME THE NEW NORMAL, NOT THE EXCEPTION

It's hard to remember a time when social media wasn't a daily ritual in my life. It's also hard to remember a time when brands weren't on social media—both in paid and organic respects—as it's become commonplace for brands to be part of our social experience. Based on the data that we've looked at in this book, it makes me think that real-time is headed in the same direction.

Within a few years we may very well see real-time marketing grow to the point that it may lose its name altogether. As brands see the low cost of entry coupled with performance bumps, it will become so commonplace that it will just be the new way of doing social, and the "real-time" label may fade away completely. Marketing, as we've discussed, will follow an audience's attention, and as that attention demands more and more relevance, RTM will become more and more just a new way to do marketing.

VERTICALS WILL SPECIALIZE TO BUILD REAL-TIME SUCCESS

As more brands embrace real-time marketing, the practice will grow in its level of sophistication. Brands will learn that the real-time audience, and the right tactics to engage with each subaudience, is not one size fits all. Social teams will learn how to make the most of the advantages or constraints that are present in each industry, and understand that "the audience" is actually made up of subgroups with very different tastes and needs. An approach that works well for a CPG brand won't necessarily work for an auto manufacturer, and real-time marketing tactics will adapt to reflect that reality.

Sports Teams and Broadcasters

While real-time marketing is new for many brands, sports teams and the networks that broadcast their games have been capitalizing on concentrations of attention for years. Peter Stringer, the Senior Director of Digital Media for the Boston Celtics, knows this better than anyone else. "Most of our Twitter activity happens when the team is in action. Whether they are practicing or playing, it's all about what's happening with that team right now," Stringer explains. "We have a built in story line during the season that creates our own moments on a daily basis. When brands are chiming in on the Super Bowl in real-time, they are trying to create relevance with the audience where it doesn't yet exist. With sports being one of the few DVR-proof programming categories left, we create those relevant moments for ourselves and know the audience is along for the ride."[1]

Sports teams have a huge opportunity with every micro-event to capitalize on the conversation and stay relevant – both for their own brands as well as sponsors. As technologies and processes emerge to take full advantage of understanding, promoting, and guiding real-time conversations within and between games, teams and players are in a great position to benefit and become even more relevant to the audience on a daily basis.

B2B

Companies that work mostly with other companies have always had an interesting use case with social media, and real-time marketing is no different. Does a corporate buyer care about the tone and voice of the brand that sends them an invoice each month? Can a medical supplier change purchasing decisions by chiming in on the Grammys, and if they do, is anyone listening? Questions like these, while valid, don't mean there's not a place for B2B brands in the RTM landscape. While a majority of real-time efforts to date have been around pop culture moments, there's nothing to say that it always has to be that way. Brands that chime in on current events that might be more top of mind in certain industries—market news, commodity prices, or innovations in the space—might find a niche and be rewarded by becoming a trusted source for industry updates. Real-time marketing is about being relevant to the audience, and if the audience's mind is on copper futures, then there's an opportunity for brands around that conversation.

Highly Regulated Industries

The growth of real-time marketing will put more pressure on highly regulated industries (pharmaceuticals, alcohol, tobacco, etc.) to find methods to stay in front of their followers. While real-time can be seen as a big risk, brands should be more willing to test the practice as it becomes more and more prominent in the marketing world and as other brands see big returns for their efforts. As we've discussed, strong processes and content guardrails are a key part of any real-time program for most brands. With highly regulated industries, having a go-to process in place is even more essential for reducing risk while still opening up the brand for reward.

REAL-TIME INTEGRATES ORGANIC AND PAID

We've talked in-depth about the organic side of RTM but haven't waded too deeply into the paid side of the equation, and no discussion around social would be complete without a mention of both sides. Paid is a huge opportunity for brands to boost their social performance around engagement, reach, and conversion, and social networks are one of the best ways to get in front of an audience with real-time content. We've seen the huge impact that increased relevance can give a brand via organic social media, and it makes sense that relevance in a paid setting can perform just as well.

Sloane Kelley is the Executive Producer of the PGA Tour Digital group and has seen success with identifying organic trends, creating relevant content, and then adding paid social media to the mix to increase the impact of effective content. "When you are able to add some dollars on top of solid RTM, it definitely acts like fuel on the fire. We've been working with the Twitter Amplify program around the delivery of PGA Tour highlights. When one of the players hits an incredible shot and we're able to get that content out to our followers that's great, but paid RTM has allowed us to get greater reach and work with a partner to sponsor the campaign. We've been really pleased with the results for video views, engagement, retweets, and favorites on Twitter."[2]

Over the next few years, the worlds of organic and paid should merge around real-time—just as they've always done with site-side advertising, search, and social. Tools should emerge that allow marketers to identify good real-time content that is resonating with the audience and quickly expand the reach of that content through paid offerings. Paid will be serve as a turbo booster when you know you've got winning RTM content that deserves even more reach.

RTM GROWTH BRINGS THE RISK OF SATURATION

Years ago I was in London working on a project for a few months, and a local news story caught my attention. A new footbridge that crossed the Thames had recently been unveiled, named the Millennium Bridge. I've walked on it since—it crosses the river right in front of the Tate Modern museum, and today functions just as a bridge should. It stands solidly in place, lets people walk on it, and gets people across the river without getting their shoes wet. But back when the bridge opened on June 10, 2000, the engineering team faced a problem with it that they hadn't anticipated.

When there were only a few people on the bridge, it held solid. But as the crowds grew, something unexpected started to happen. You see, the engineers had assumed that people walk in random patterns and that the vibrations from all those steps would essentially cancel each other out. But as the crowds grew larger and larger, vibrations built up that caused the bridge to sway just slightly side to side. Instead of walking randomly, the pedestrians were now unknowingly adjusting their steps to accommodate for the swaying, causing everyone on the bridge to walk in step, together. The vibrations from this massive force of thousands of people walking in step caused the bridge to sway uncontrollably. The bridge was closed almost immediately—it was no longer safe to travel on. Too many people walking in step caused the engineers to have to return to the drawing board, and eventually reopen the bridge years later.

Real-time marketing faces similar risks as it gains popularity. The danger of too many brands overloading a tent-pole event or an everyday trend to the point of saturation needs to be watched, studied, and kept top of mind for all real-time brands. If marketers overload the #Oscars feed with brand messages, they may lose the asset they are trying to capitalize on in the first place—the audience.

But smart brands will learn to break step, understand when an event is oversaturated and therefore not something to jump into at that moment, and differentiate themselves from others as RTM evolves. Even in a crowded real-time space, brands will still be able to find ways to grab attention—whether that is through the quickness of their response, consistently creating great content that the audience responds to, or finding a unique approach to RTM. There's always the opportunity for brands to excel. But remember, keep an eye on the RTM landscape and make sure you're not just walking in lockstep with the crowd.

THE FUTURE OF THE REAL-TIME PROCESS

As marketers work to become more in the moment each year, the processes that social teams use to jump on relevant topics will also evolve. Internal pressures, like improved expectations and processes, as well as external factors, such as new tools and opportunities where RTM can take place, will impact how brands stay in front of the crowd over the next few years.

Based on the same categories we defined for our Data-Driven RTM Process earlier in the book, here's a quick look at how the future might change our understanding and sophistication of People, Process, Technology, and Data for real-time marketing.

PEOPLE

A decade ago, it was rare to have a full-time social media team. It was a side gig for most practitioners—usually people who had raised their hands to help out on the side because they knew how to use Facebook or had over five hundred followers on Twitter. When social was in its infancy, so were the brand teams that supported it. But as social has earned more attention from audiences, brands have followed with more sophisticated teams to support their efforts. To lead social media today, people need skill sets that are very specific to the practice—not only experience on the ins and outs of each platform, but experience in paid social practices and terminology, social listening and analytics, brand guidelines and copywriting, and years of experience with a very specific toolsets to create, post, monitor, and learn from a company's social efforts. With maturity comes a higher bar, and that's exactly where real-time marketing is headed as well.

Social Media Teams Will Become More Specialized

Today as we build out our teams for big tent-pole events, brands and agencies are repurposing people from across the organization who 1) they think could do a good job, 2) have expressed interest or 3) are available that day. This will change as digital marketers throughout the industry get more and more RTM under their belt, and specialized roles will emerge not only around real-time marketing but also in tent-pole events versus everyday RTM. These skills may emerge within the social teams themselves, but the days of having someone on the team without real-time experience are coming to an end.

Social Media Teams Will Become More Empowered

Do you remember when you had just turned 16 and you wanted to take the car out for the first time? If you were like me, you shyly approached your dad and asked if you could borrow the car keys, but you promised you wouldn't be more than an hour, you just had this thing you had to do, and not a scratch, I swear, not a scratch. Well, that's a similar scenario to the first time brands wanted to Tweet in real-time without someone in Legal approving the copy and image—you were happy just to have a little bit of freedom, and if things went well, you didn't scratch your social media wheels before pulling back in the garage. But the second time you asked for the keys, and the third and the twentieth, it got a bit easier each time for both sides. You came to the conversation with a bit more confidence—you knew what you were doing, and you, hopefully, had a good track record of success to go along with it. And your dad knew that because his car wasn't in the middle of a lake, you could probably be trusted a bit more each time. As social media teams get more seasoned with their experience around RTM, many of the processes and checkpoints will fade as both sides grow more comfortable. This means more freedom for social media teams to execute in the ways they want to (but still within guidelines), and should result in better returns for their organizations.

Social Media Teams Will Grow Stronger Links to the Brand Team

Responding in the moment demands that social teams be fully immersed in the brand voice, tone, and guidelines. They need to be able to answer a question, in the voice of the brand, in their sleep, knowing that any mistakes they make can be shared across the Twittersphere. As more brands engage in RTM, especially everyday RTM, no one in the organization will know the brand better than the real-time marketing team. Bridges will form, if they haven't already, between the Brand team and the Social Media team, and the two may ultimately converge within certain corporate structures. The closer the two groups can coordinate and be aligned, the better, and organizations that push for these connections should see a benefit in real-time marketing performance.

PROCESS

Process, when done right, is never a static thing. It nudges here and there based on the best way to meet the goal—it needs to be understood and repeatable, but also flexible and adaptive to a changing environment. Well, social media is the very definition of a changing environment, and with every new social media channel, event, marketing tactic, and technology innovation, a process that is set in stone will start looking old and ineffective pretty fast. Real-time marketing processes should change as time goes by, but what will this change look like? I can see a few areas where the process will shift, improve, and become optimized.

RTM Processes Will Be Built with a Goals-Driven Approach

We talked about starting a real-time process with goals, but this isn't done with every brand today. If brands adopt this practice early, they'll be at an advantage, knowing what they're trying to accomplish and building tactics and content around their primary goals. But for some, goals will evolve as the second, third, or fourth real-time effort completes. At some point, social media teams (or their bosses) will start asking, "What are we trying to accomplish here?" the same way goals have evolved in digital and social after brief experimental periods. Reason usually prevails, even in marketing.

RTM Processes Will Be Refined, Not Built in a Day

There's one thing teams can be sure of: the first time they define a real-time marketing process, they'll get it wrong. Not the whole thing, but certain parts. They'll leave out a step. They'll forget to include Mark from PR because he was gone the day the team did the brainstorm. They'll be left without knowing how to respond to certain micro-events and feel they missed an opportunity. Unexpected things will happen, and that's... expected. The process will become refined, but it will take time. Different experiences with RTM will highlight different weaknesses in the process, and pieces will get rebuilt to become better and better each time.

RTM Will Become an Everyday Process, Not an Event

RTM is widely recognized as a strategy for large events, but is just now starting to gain recognition as an everyday social tactic. As marketers learn the power of being in the moment every day, and have performance gains to show for their efforts, more brands should begin making RTM an everyday practice within their organizations. It will be a win on both sides of the equation—audiences will see more relevant conversations around topics and trends they are interested in, and in return brands and media companies will see an increase in engagement and sharing by their followers.

RTM Tactics Will Become More Recognizable by Brand

As any practice becomes more widely adopted throughout an industry, all players can start to look the same. We've witnessed the explosive growth that RTM is seeing with some of the world's largest brands, and as this trend continues and real-time becomes the industry norm, companies face the risk of looking like the competition all over again. As almost every industry has experienced, more players bring the need for more differentiation. Brands will find their own unique ways of not only being relevant to the audience but also using tactics that are known as watermarks for their specific brands. We've seen DiGiorno's all-caps Tweets stick out even in a crowded tent-pole event, and J. C. Penney's showing that creating an underlying "Tweeting with Mittens" story line can help bring attention to their real-time efforts. This evolution should be a win for brands as long as the differentiation is true to the brand and isn't just an awkward attempt to gain a short-term burst of attention.

TECHNOLOGY

The newest technology, by definition, is always evolving and many of the platforms we use for marketing today hadn't even been written on a whiteboard a decade ago. Technology seems to come in two different forms: incremental advances to satisfy customer requests and solutions to problems that customers had never even considered. Advances in real-time tools should take both forms—as the practice matures, tools will make everyday tasks and process easier, faster, better, and more measurable. But we'll also see advances in technology to utilize real-time and become relevant to the audience in ways we hadn't expected. Here are a few examples that fall somewhere in the middle.

RTM Technology Will Be Built to Identify Trends and Alert brands

It would be great to have the budget and resources for a fully staffed social media war room full of experts who can identify the latest micro-trend, every day. I'm picturing a *War Games*-type NORAD center with 50 highly trained experts monitoring giant screens with every trend under the sun displayed, ready to discover, curate, and select the right trends for the business to engage with. The reality of the situation, as anyone in the industry can tell you, is much less sophisticated and has a much, much lower budget to match. But we don't need experts to find these trends every time. Tools and their associated algorithms can do this job for us. Technology will emerge that understands what a brand is interested in and that can identify emerging micro-trends to match the brand's content criteria. Algorithms can detect when a term is about to trend, when to act, and most importantly, send alerts to the right team members so they don't have to be staring at a screen all day. The result of these technologies will be a social media team that makes better use of its time, while still getting the performance benefits of jumping in on in-the-moment trends and conversations.

RTM Technology Will Be Built to Identify Topic Saturation

Remember the Millennium Bridge from earlier in this chapter? Tools will be built to help brands figure out when jumping on to a trend isn't the right way to go, and when diminishing returns might be kicking in either due to too much branded content on a certain subject, or just too much social content from a specific brand within a given timeline. Tools like these will help social media teams be smarter about RTM, and bring data to the concept that sometimes a brand just needs to keep quiet.

RTM Technology Will Evolve to Understand Optimal Tactics

For the past few decades, smart marketers have been testing different tactics to see what resonates with their audience. With real-time marketing, the tactics used should evolve in similar fashion, and technology will help pave the way to bring a data-driven approach to finding methods that work. Social media teams will test different tactics to see what resonates and which copy, creative, and overall approaches to RTM are effective for their audience. Brands will learn the best methods (punctuation, sentence form), media (pictures? video? just text?), timing, and other factors that help their real-time marketing provide optimal results. Approaches that work in other forms of marketing won't necessarily work in social, and many social practices used by brands today won't be a fit for getting the most out of RTM. Brands will learn and evolve, and tools will help them measure the effectiveness of each tactic, resulting in better content and smarter marketing in the moment.

Manish Mehta is the Chief Product Officer for Spredfast, and he offers this insight into where real-time marketing technology is headed: "With the amount of data we have today, the technology should evolve to understand what patterns work better than others for specific brands and make recommendations based on different factors. With solid data science, we can identify trends as they arise and score each for specific characteristics: audience, subject matter, lifecycle of the trend, and more. By alerting brands when there's a solid match, we can leverage technology to increase the probability of success and the best moments to engage in real-time marketing."[3]

RTM Technology Will Evolve to Understand Which Brands Are Performing Best

Tools and technology can not only show a brand how their real-time efforts are performing, but they can also provide data and insights into how other RTM brands are seeing success. Tools will emerge that allow marketers to look at the RTM efforts of a competitive set over time to recognize effective tactics, see the best brands across the globe that are participating in Trending Topics, and get a view of all the RTM happening during a given tent-pole event. Brands with this type of data, and good analysts who can quickly process the information to provide actionable insights, will only improve the quality and impact of real-time marketing across every event and daily trend.

RTM Technology Will Move Consumers down the Funnel

Throughout this book, we've looked at RTM and its impact on social engagement, but engagement is only the beginning. All social brands have an end goal in mind, and that goal generally revolves around bringing in more customers or making their current customers more valuable. The performance of real-time has shown us the huge impact it has had on engagement, and smart marketers will turn the corner to create more and more direct revenue opportunities with in-the-moment marketing.

Manish Tripathi is Assistant Professor of Marketing at Goizueta Business School at Emory University, and specializes in marketing analytics. He believes that as the practice of RTM gets more sophisticated, it will bring with it the ability to increase revenue and boost customer lifetime value. Engagement is a great start, but this data builds out the opportunity to create more optimized, personalized offers that will resonate with consumers.

"Let's say we go back ten years—if we were discussing real-time marketing back then, we would be talking about using data from the customer about some action that just took place and giving them a more relevant offer based on that event. I could present them with some sort of message or offer that would help raise awareness, increase sales, impact whatever my goal is. Over the past few years, a new component has emerged with this rise of RTM that allows a marketer to understand that a consumer is interested and engaged in a certain topic or event, and this can all happen as the event is taking place. If we fast-forward a few years, the main question will be how do I create an offer that combines all these different pieces of data—maybe it's mobile data that knows I just walked into a store or additional social data that knows I just commented on a brand's page on Facebook—and combine that with the knowledge of what is top of mind for a consumer in that moment. When you take that data set and then add all the other CRM data that we have about that consumer, we'll be able to create highly-personalized, highly-relevant messages like we've never seen before that can have precision in both their accuracy and timeliness of the message."[4]

With these new opportunities, brands will need to remember that balancing commerce and relationships is still a mix of art and science, and that just because hypertargeted offers are a possibility within the framework of RTM, it might not make sense to do so every day or with every Tweet.

DATA

As marketers adapt to an increasingly more real-time world, the availability of data, and the demand for more information will increase in step. New technologies will make data more abundant, and smarter teams will be hungry for proof points to measure their findings, learn more about the competition, and find the next relevant trend to chime in on. What will the major shift in RTM data look like over the next few years?

Real-Time Data Will Be Available in Real-Time

Shocking, I know, but RTM data today doesn't always exist in an environment in which the team can easily access the most up-to-date information. Teams spend a lot of time hitting "refresh" on their browser, getting screens to reload, and searching through multiple windows for the latest conversations around a topic. As marketing becomes more in the moment, the data will need to follow. Tools that access real-time data for brands will rise to the top, and brands will have access to the right information at the right time to make the call on RTM.

The explosion of social TV, the experience of using social media while simultaneously watching a television broadcast, will only boost the need and opportunity for real-time data. Shawndra Hill is Professor of Operations and Information Management at the Wharton School at the University of Pennsylvania and heads up their Social TV Lab, and believes that advertising will help fuel the real-time need for data. "People are responding in real-time to what's happening on television, and there's a huge opportunity to get people engaged in real-time with brands if you use the right tactics and tools. Consumers and viewers are coming to expect real-time engagement with shows more and more. As the culture changes towards having the audience become more involved, the opportunity for advertisers to pay attention to what people are watching is huge. If you know that someone is watching *The Voice* because they have revealed that via social media, then brands can, in real-time, target that audience accordingly."[5]

Real-Time Data Will Include Additional Data Sources

Moments are not just happening within the world of social media, and there's additional data that can help paint the full picture of each trend. In the social TV world alone, broadcasters hold a huge amount of data that can help tell the story of a moment, including programming information, minute-by-minute ratings, and tune-in by geographic region.

Jason Burby, President of the Americas at POSSIBLE, the largest digital agency in the WPP family, sees mobile as a data source that holds a huge amount of potential value for RTM. Mobile data, providing highly detailed geolocation data among other dimensions, can give marketers even more tools to use in order to reach their audience at the right time, with the right message. "If you look at social media's capacity to identify trends and understand what's relevant, and then you add the additional data that a mobile device can report, you create an environment where conversations can become hyper-relevant." But still, for Burby, the allure of new technology shouldn't overshadow the fundamentals of any good campaign. "The companies that succeed will be the ones that are thinking of their overall strategy, defining success up front, and making sure the conversation is relevant for the audience. If those factors are front-and-center, everything else will fall into place with the right team."[6]

Real-Time Social Data Will Be More Targeted

Today in many channels, the message that goes out through organic social channels is one-size-fits-all. Paid social offerings allow for increased targeting based on interest-graph and demographic dimensions, and the organic side of the house should eventually take the same path. In the future, brands should be able to create multiple messages for subaudiences within their larger audience, and have an even better opportunity to deliver the right message to the right group.

Real-Time Social Data Will Be More Robust

As the practice of RTM gains more traction, social networks will encourage the process by providing richer data. Brands can make better decisions with more data dimensions at their fingertips, and social networks can provide better information as they build out tools for marketers to quickly access and analyze the data. More robust impression data—knowing not only how many users engaged with an organic piece of social content but also how many actually saw it, will drive a more complete picture of success. Demographic information will empower brands with not only how many people are talking about a topic but also a deeper understanding of how that audience overlaps with the brand's target. If 10,000 people are discussing the NFL Draft, but the majority of them are men aged 45+, MTV will probably not be interested in jumping into that discussion.

CHANGE IS GOOD

As RTM evolves, brands will become better at the practice and more empowered to act in the moment. Data will play a huge part in this transformation, validating the power of relevancy and activating more and more companies to seize moments.

This page intentionally left blank

Chapter 9

CONCLUSION

FOR YEARS NOW, SOCIAL MEDIA LEADERS have been asked to take on some pretty groundbreaking tasks. Brands and agencies have recognized huge shifts of audience attention heading to social networks, and these teams have been asked to stay in front of them every step of the way. A new social network just popped up—make sure we have a presence. There's a big event coming up—make sure we have a point of view. All this is done to stay in the right place at the right time with the right message, and remain relevant to their audience.

These social media teams have been asked to become Masters of the Known—to make the most of a channel or conversation that involves them. There are a few hundred customers talking to us on Facebook, so let's go figure out how to make the most of that conversation. There are a few thousand tweets about our new product, so let's go figure out whether people like it or they don't. Our web traffic is down—how do we find out which referral source needs more advertising budget? These teams have been asked to tackle known problems with creative and efficient solutions to make the most of each new platform and stay ahead of the curve.

But now brands are discovering that the Known isn't enough anymore. What a few smart social teams are discovering is that to truly stay relevant to their audience, they need to evolve become Masters of the Unknown. They need to be able to react at a moment's notice to the latest breaking news, Trending Topic, or micro-event, just like their followers. The pace of conversation has amplified, and pumping out the same pre-canned messaging doesn't always resonate with the modern consumer.

Hopefully, through this book, you've learned that to truly become a Master of the Unknown, you'll need a good set of people, process, technology, and data to give you an advantage. I hope you've learned how social data can empower your team to be more creative, and how a goals-driven approach can help keep a chaotic practice pointed in the right direction for business results. I hope you've learned that real-time marketing hasn't finished evolving, and that smart brands will need to continue to innovate and stay relevant. And I hope that you've discovered that in most cases, brands are being welcomed into social conversations. All of these discoveries translate to new opportunities that brands can leverage every day.

As real-time marketing grows and matures, I hope it will benefit both sides—the brands and consumers. If brands can see better results from making content and offers more relevant to each individual, then that's a win for marketing departments across the world. If consumers can receive timely messages about something that is both top of mind and valuable to them, then they can find a benefit from this evolution as well. So long as companies keep relevance top of mind, I believe we'll be trending in the right direction. Luckily, the data agrees.

NOTES

1   RELEVANCE IS TRENDING UP

1. Lieb, Rebecca. Interview with Rebecca Lieb. Via phone, March 20, 2014
2. Ibid.
3. Ibid.

2   UNDERSTANDING BRANDS ON TWITTER

1. "Best Global Brands 2013—List View," Interbrand, accessed June 6, 2014, http://www.interbrand.com/en/best-global-brands/2013/top-100-list-view.aspx.
2. Sterne, Jim. Interview with Jim Sterne. Via phone, March 26, 2014.

6   AIMING FOR REAL-TIME SUCCESS

1. Barry Cunningham. Interview with Barry Cunningham. Via phone, March 19, 2014.

7   THE DATA-DRIVEN RTM PROCESS

1. Josh Martin. Interview with Josh Martin. Via phone, April 23, 2014.
2. Rod Strother. Interview with Rod Strother. Via phone, April 21, 2014.

8   THE FUTURE OF RTM

1. Peter Stringer. Interview with Peter Stringer. Via phone, May 13, 2014.
2. Sloane Kelley. Interview with Sloane Kelley. Via phone, May 30, 2014.
3. Manish Mehta. Interview with Manish Mehta. Austin TX, June 11, 2014.
4. Manish Tripathi. Interview with Manish Tripathi. Via phone, May 14, 2014.
5. Shawndra Hill. Interview with Shawndra Hill. Via phone, May 22, 2014.
6. Jason Burby. Interview with Jason Burby. Via phone, May 5, 2014.

This page intentionally left blank

INDEX